Checkmate for Children

Kevin Stark

Checkmate for Children

Mastering the Most Important Skill in Chess

New In Chess 2010

© 2010 New In Chess
Published by New In Chess, Alkmaar, The Netherlands
www.newinchess.com

Cover design: Volken Beck
Translation: Peter Boel
Correction: Steve Giddins
Supervisor: Peter Boel
Proofreading: René Olthof
Production: Anton Schermer

ISBN: 978-90-5691-309-0

Contents

Part III

Part IV

Necessary Conditions

This is a chess book for pure beginners, who have only just learned the moves, and hardly have any practical knowledge. The only thing that is required is a solid **knowledge of the movements of the pieces**, and of the **basic rules**. A knowledge of the elementary endgames King + Rook versus King, and King + Queen versus King, is helpful when you start with this book, but not absolutely necessary.

It is, however, necessary before you start, to learn the chess notation, as well as a few special concepts like rank, file and diagonal. This knowledge will be provided in the first chapter. In fact, many children will probably not really like this part, but it is highly important for all forms of regular training. Besides, only with knowledge of the notation will you be able to use chess books of all kinds!

This book is useful for **chess beginners of all age categories**, although, of course, very young chess friends will require the help and support of their parents, their brother or sister or, for example, a trainer.

A **chessboard with chess pieces** should be close at hand, so that the user can set up positions from the book on the board and have a closer look at them. Adult readers will be able to solve most of the exercises from the diagrams, but with difficult positions, which will come soon after the simple basics, looking at them on a chessboard will be closer to practice as well as helpful and desirable.

It is not advisable to study the majority of positions in the book with a computer. Of course, you can now and then enter a position into a chess program and analyse it with the help of the computer. But nothing can replace the act of simply looking at the chessboard. This contributes strongly to the development of a subconscious feel for the position and for the game. This especially holds true for novice children.

Even if you already have some knowledge of the game, you should work through this book from beginning to end. Systematic training is important, and a possible repetition or refreshment of certain pieces of knowledge already present, has never done anybody any harm! This applies especially to adult beginners, who often want to make rapid progress and in so doing miss several important basic concepts. This is only human and understandable, but it often leads to annoying problems at a later stage.

If you follow these suggestions, you will rapidly learn a lot about tactics, and you will soon be able to apply this knowledge in your games.

Introduction

According to the basic rules, tactics are the most important and most fundamental element in chess. You have to know the properties of the individual pieces, and the way they cooperate, if you want to win a chess game. Tactics occur in all phases of a chess game, from the first opening moves to the endgame.

In this book we start with a systematic training in tactics for beginners, who do not have any prior knowledge whatsoever. Most of these will be children or teenagers, but this book can be used by beginners of all age categories. First, we will have a look at the so-called 'chess notation', the method for recording chess moves and chess games. This is indispensible knowledge for working further with this – and in fact any other – chess book. A pupil should have a solid command of the chess notation. This will also help him to have a better view of the chessboard, and practice shows that a good learning of the notation at an early stage also helps you to play better and more successfully later on.

We will look piece by piece how each individual piece can give mate to the opponent's king. True, a beginner will mostly lose at an early stage in the game, when mate is still far off, but to give mate is the goal of every chess game, and we must first of all get to know that goal a little better. How can we ever expect to win a chess game, if we don't know which position we should strive for as our goal? Moreover, the mating exercises will sharpen your eye for the way the individual pieces operate, and for their possibilities. By and by, certain important concepts will also be explained, enabling the pupil to widen his knowledge while he is playing.

Next, after the elementary mating positions, we will learn how to produce a mate in 2 or 3 moves and with more than one piece – in other words, here we already learn to create certain small combinations on the chessboard. This training method was developed in the Soviet chess school during the 1920s, and it is still successfully applied today. This systematic make-up ensures that all important positions, the so-called 'motifs' or 'mating pattern', can be recognized and applied by the pupil. Therefore it is important to work through the book from beginning to end and not 'jump' from one subject to another, for this might be at the expense of certain important knowledge.

We start every chapter with a general introduction, then we show further examples and deepen the acquired information by means of a small quiz. Learning is more important than solving, but you should re-read the chapter if there are many exercises you have not solved, or if you have made too many mistakes in your solutions.

If your results don't improve, you should consider extra training with the learning material we recommend on page 139. Very young children may not yet be ready for systematic chess training, or they may be unable to summon the motivation for it at a given moment. In such cases it is best to simply wait a while and then try again. Sometimes just a few weeks or months can work miracles for children!

I wish you a lot of fun with this tactics training.

Kevin Stark

Chess Notation –
this is where it all starts!

Beginners often shy away from learning the chess notation. 'I don't like this, do I have to?', many a youngster will grumble.

Have no fear, you will quite quickly get used to it. And yes, you do have to, since otherwise you could not read this or any other chess book, nor could you play through a game and so train further and improve at chess. And you could never show anyone your fantastic victory, which – provided that you practise diligently and play with concentration – you will certainly gain soon! For us, chess notation is what notes are to music: we won't get anywhere without it!

Besides, for most of you the chess notation will already be familiar. If you have ever played Battleships, you almost know it already!

On our chessboard every vertical line gets a letter (a, b, c...), and every horizontal line a number (1, 2, 3...). And if we want to indicate a certain point on the board, we only have to mention the letter and the number and already anyone can see where this point is on the chessboard (more advanced players can see it in their heads). Now, instead of elaborate terms like 'that square up in the corner on the left', we can simply indicate 'a8' and anyone can see or imagine what we mean.

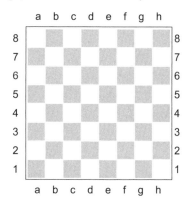

The chessboard on the left shows us the letters and numbers that are affixed on the sides of all boards used in tournaments. The board on the right shows all the squares with their 'names'. Thus, if you are in doubt, you can always check whether you have indicated the right square.

Actually, now we could already write any chess move by indicating the starting square and the goal square with our 'code'. But in order to make it yet a little easier and more accessible, we add the name of the piece before it. Only the pawn misses out – it doesn't get any identification. Of course we abbreviate the name of every piece, otherwise it would become too long. We use the following signs and abbreviations:

King	♔	= K
Queen	♕	= Q
Rook	♖	= R
Bishop	♗	= B
Knight	♘	= N
Pawn	♙	—

Let's try this out. In the diagram on the left the white king is standing on the **e1**-square.

If he wants to attack the black rook, he moves towards it – to **f1**.

We add the sign **K** for the king before the move, and separate the indicated starting square (e1) and the goal square (f1) with a hyphen.

So, our move is called ♔**e1-f1**.

Quite easy, wasn't it?

What do we call the move by the white rook, when it moves to the square next to the king?

And if the white pawn in the centre moves forward, what do we call this move?[1]

To avoid confusion we number the moves throughout the game. So we start with the first move for White, which is often with his king's pawn: 1.e2-e4. If Black is to move, this is indicated by 1...; in our example this is 1...e7-e5. There are a number of further signs and additions, e.g. for capturing, giving check, giving mate, etc., and we will have a look at them on the next page.

---

1   The rook move is called ♖a1-d1 and the pawn move d4-d5. With a pawn move we don't put a sign before the names of the squares.

Further symbols:

If a piece is captured, instead of a hyphen, an **x** is given, i.e., **x = captures**.[2]

Kingside (or short) castling is indicated by **0-0**.

Queenside (or long) castling is indicated by **0-0-0**.

Capturing a pawn 'en passant' (i.e. in passing) is indicated by adding **e.p.** after the pawn move. (*We will return to this concept further on and will then explain it in more detail.*)

If a check is given, we indicate this by **+**.

For mate we use **#**. In older books this is sometimes indicated by **++**; but in this book we use this sign to indicate a double check.

In chess books or chess magazines where games or fragments are reproduced, some **assessments** and **comments** are included for the reader.

For example, a **?** after a move means that this was a **weak move**.

Logically, two question marks mean that the move was still weaker: **??**

(Mostly in such cases, the move isn't twice as bad as normal, but it is very stupid, e.g. the queen was left en prise, or mate on the next move is missed.)

Of course there are also **strong moves**.

They are characterized by **!**, and if it was a very good, maybe even a brilliant move, we give it two exclamation marks: **!!**

There are more signs for the assessment of moves, and also for the assessment of positions, but we do not need to know them at the start of this course.

Below we give a short overview of the most important signs for moves and comments:

0-0	= kingside (short) castling
0-0-0	= queenside (long) castling
+	= check
++	= double check
#	= checkmate
?	= a weak move, mistake
??	= a grave mistake
!	= a strong move
!!	= a very strong move

---

2   Older chess books often use a colon instead of an **'x'**, for example:
3.d4:e5. The meaning is the same.

Files, Ranks and Diagonals

In addition to the chess notation we have to spend some time on a few technical terms – please, don't be impatient and have a look at these as well!

The vertical, horizontal and diagonal lines on the chessboard each have their own special names.

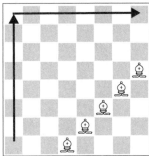

- The vertical lines on the chessboard (thin arrow) are called **'files'**.
- The horizontal lines (bold arrow) are called **'ranks'**.
- The diagonal lines (indicated in the diagram by the white bishops) are called **'diagonals'**.
- The file names correspond with the letters on the edge of the board, so in our example the 'a-file' is indicated.
- The ranks get their designation from the numbers. So in our example we have the '8th rank'.
- The diagonals are named after their starting squares and end squares, so in our example we have the 'd1-h5 diagonal'. The shortest diagonals are the ones from a2-b1/a7-b8 and their opposites on the other side of the board. The **longest diagonals** are the ones from a1-h8/h1-a8, which are called 'long diagonals'.

And now we will do a little test, to see if you have understood everything correctly:
A rook on c1 is standing on the ...-**file** and on the ... **rank**.
If two white rooks are standing on the next-to-last horizontal line (from White's point of view), they are standing on the ...
The white bishop on e2 in the above diagram is standing on the ... from ... to ...
Bishops exclusively move along ..., rooks move along ... and ...
Pawns cannot leave their ..., except when they capture. But with every turn they move one ... forward, and on the first move they may even move two ... forward.

Have you got all this? We will see on the next page.

Exercise: Who is standing where?

	The
	white king
	black rook
	white rook's pawn
	white bishop
	black knight
	black king
	knight in the corner
	black pawn

Small test on the previous page:

A rook on c1 is standing on the *c*-file and the *1st* rank. The two white rooks are on the *7th rank*. The white bishop is standing on the *diagonal from a6 to f1* (or the other way round), and it is also on the diagonal from d1 to h5. Bishops move along diagonals, rooks along *ranks* and *files*. Pawns cannot leave their *file* and move forward one *rank*, on the first move possibly two *ranks*.

Solutions Exercise
'Who is standing where?'

white king	c1
black rook	d4
white rook's pawn	h5
whitebishop	g2
black knight	c7
black king	g8
knight in the corner	a1

If you have **6 correct answers**, you can start with the tactical training. One mistake or oversight could happen to any experienced player as well.

If you have made **two mistakes**, think what may be the cause of this. Perhaps you have misunderstood something? Please have another look at the above material!

If you have made three or more mistakes, start again from the beginning. Don't be,sad – the chess notation is really important and you should master it before you start with the training!

Part I – Typical Mating Patterns with One Piece

Each piece and each pawn on the chessboard can give check or checkmate to the opponent's king – except of course the kings themselves, who are, after all, not allowed to touch each other. The properties of the pieces are obviously quite different due to their strengths and the way they move. For example, for the mighty queen, helped by her king, it is easy to give mate, whereas the knight cannot do this at all without more support – not even a pair of knights together can give mate by force.

It is important that we know what the individual mating positions, also called **'mating patterns'** or **'mating motifs'**, look like, and what the strengths and weaknesses of our pieces are.

Firstly, in the given exercises you are almost always asked to give mate in 1 move. However, by and by we will sometimes make things a little more complicated, and we will also show a few positions where the mate may take a few more moves.

• Notation in bold (e.g. **1.♖a1-a8#**) indicates the main variation of the solution (also called text variation). Alternatives, i.e. other possible moves, are indicated by moves in normal print (e.g., 1.♔e1-f1).
• Moves in bold italics (e.g. ***1.♖g3-g8+***) mark the beginning of an alternative **solution**, or of another interesting variation.
• Sometimes a piece can give mate in two different ways from the starting point. We will indicate this in abridged form (e.g., **1.♕d5-b7/g8#**).
• Unless explicitly stated otherwise, it is always White's turn to move. This is indicated by a small white square under the diagram.
• **W/B** under a diagram means that both sides have a tactical opportunity and you are required to find the solution for both sides.

Every mating pattern starts with an introduction, which demonstrates typical mate situations. This is followed by a quiz where, in addition to modified versions of the demonstrated mating patterns, new, as yet unknown positions, are also shown. It is not the aim of the quiz that you solve as many exercises as possible, but that you have a go at the positions, you look for solutions without help and – regardless whether the exercise is solved or not – learn from the solutions with their extensive comments. The reader will be better able to remember a solution he has found himself than one that is brought to him on a silver plate and, above all, he will improve his understanding of the principles underlying the solutions.

If you cannot find the solution to an exercise, it's best to look it up in the solution part in the back of the book and then continue with the next position.

Mate with the Rook

The rook **cannot** give mate to the opponent's king on its own. It needs the help of another piece or its king.

Moreover, the rook can only give mate to a king that is **on the edge of the board**.

Since no king may walk into a check, every king has a kind of 'protection zone' around him, which cannot be entered by the enemy king. We can see this in *D1*. The marked squares around the white king make up his protection zone.

D1 The protection zone of the king

In *D1* the white king is standing directly opposite his enemy. We call this situation **'opposition'**. The white king's protection zone deprives his opponent of three out of his five possible escape squares (g4, g5, g6). Therefore, the latter can only move on the h-file, to the squares h4 or h6.

If the white king isn't directly opposite his enemy (i.e., they are not standing in opposition), the black king can escape to the side (*D2*).

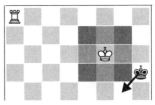

D2 The white king does not have the opposition

Now we have learned everything we have to know about the mate with King + Rook:
- The opponent's king must be at the edge of the board;
- Our own king must be standing right opposite the enemy king (in opposition).

Then, if the rook gives check from a safe distance (arrow), where it cannot be captured, then we immediately have **mate**, as is shown in *D3*.

All the squares where the black king could go to, are controlled by the rook. There is no escape – MATE!

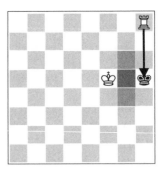

D3 Mating position

Of course, this mate is not only possible at the side edge, but also at the upper and lower edges of the board (i.e. the back ranks), as shown in the next two diagrams *D4* and *D5*:

D4 Mate on Black's back rank

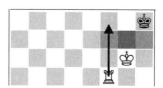

D5 Mate on White's back rank

It is even easier when the enemy king is standing in the corner (*D6/D7*), since in that case our king does not have to have the opposition. The reason is quite simple: the black king cannot escape to the side. The hole in our protection zone (*see the marked squares*) lies outside the board. Again, this position can occur in the left hand or the right hand corner, and upwards or sidewards.

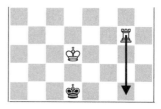

D6 The king in the corner

D7 Mate on the h-file

The mate becomes even easier if the opponent also has a pawn (*D8*) or a piece (*D9*) that blocks his escape square. In that case we can also win in positions where the mate would otherwise be far away or perhaps even impossible. In our examples Black's own pieces prevent their king from escaping via h7 or a2 respectively.

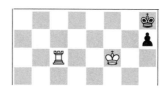

D8 The pawn blocks the h7-square

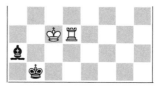

D9 The bishop blocks the a2-square

Quiz 1: Mate with the Rook

In all the exercises White is to move, and he must – if possible – immediately give mate to the black king. Some of the exercises are already a little more complicated than our examples, but that shouldn't be a problem.

Always look which squares the protection zone of the white king is taking from the opponent. Also look which other squares the latter cannot move to. This way you will recognize if the black king can be mated, and how. A small tip: not every exercise requires you to give mate in one move – otherwise it would be much too simple and boring! This will also be the case in the other quizzes in this book. Sometimes they contain a few such 'special' positions. It doesn't really matter if you cannot solve these at the first stroke.

And now, good luck with our first test!

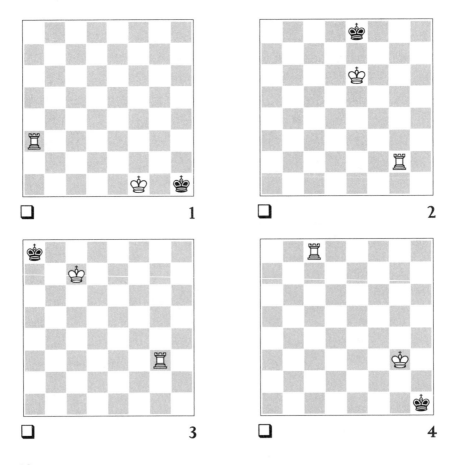

❑   1   ❑   2

❑   3   ❑   4

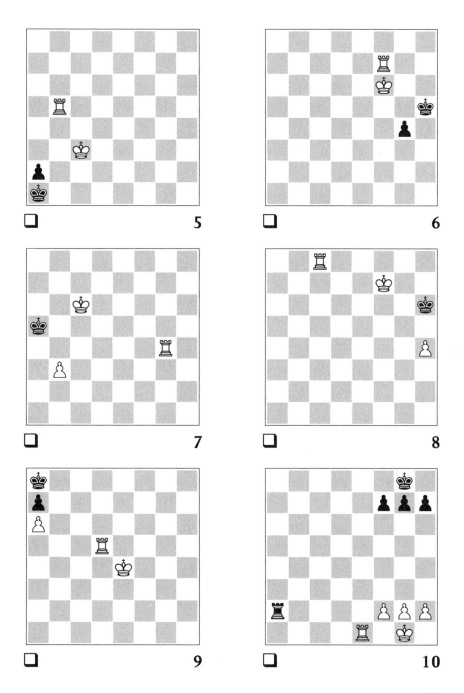

5

6

7

8

9

10

Solutions to 'Mate with the Rook'

1	We throttle the king in the corner with **1.♖a3-h3#!**
2	And push the king over the edge with **1.♖g2-g8#!**
3	Here two checks are possible, but only one of them is strong: **1.♖g3-a3#**. Not every check wins, even with the king in the corner: after *1.♖g3-g8+?* the king escapes to a7. Now the mate takes a little longer: 1...♔a8-a7 2.♖g8-g6 Blocks the king's escape and forces him to move to the corner. After 2...♔a7-a8 we have a mating position again: *3.♖g6-a6#*.
4	Here also we have to pay attention: while **1.♖c8-c1#** wins right away, instead *1.♖c8-h8+* ♔h1-g1 does not lead to an immediate mate.
5	This time you cannot give mate immediately – you also have to pay attention: **1.♖b5-d5** (or to one of the next squares) **1...♔a1-b1 2.♖d5-d1#** [after *1.♖b5-b6??* or other moves by the rook on b2-b8, Black is **stalemated**!! More about this on the next page!]
6	Here his own pawn takes the escape square g4 away from the king. This is sad for Black, because now he loses by **1.♖f7-h7#**.
7	This time the rook can venture closer to the king, since it is protected by its pawn on b3: **1.♖g4-a4#**.
8	The protection zone of the white king does not suffice to lock up the black king, but the h4 pawn takes over this job by controlling the escape square g5. Therefore, **1.♖c8-h8#**.
9	Even without support from its king, the rook can give mate, if the enemy king is hemmed in by a pawn of his own and one of the opponent. The escape squares a7 and b7 are blocked, and thus, **1.♖d5-d8#** wins easily. A white pawn on c6 (instead of a6) would lead to the same result.
10	If the enemy king has no escape square (also called '**luft**') in a castled position, the rook can give a typical back rank mate: **1.♖e1-e8#**.

Well, that wasn't so hard, was it?

And with this test you have also learned several new mating possibilities. On the next page you will find out what 'stalemate' is all about, and after that we will have a look at mating patterns with two rooks.

Stalemate

If a player is to move, is not in check, cannot play with his king and cannot play with any other piece either, he is stalemated. The game is considered undecided (draw), no matter who stood better or who had more material. Both players receive half a point.

Just like mate, stalemate automatically means the end of the game. Sometimes it happens that both players do not notice stalemate (or mate) and play on, only noticing it many moves later. Then the stalemate (or the mate) is declared valid with retrospective effect. After all, the players have continued a game that was already finished according to the rules, and so none of the further moves have any significance.

In *D1* Black, if it is his move, is stalemated.
The pawn cannot move any further, his king cannot move into a check, and therefore all the conditions for stalemate are fulfilled. If White is to move and he moves his rook along the b-file, it will still be stalemate (except, of course, in case of 1.♖b5-b1+??). All the king moves on the c- or d-file also maintain the stalemate situation.
Only ♔c3-b3 (or ♔c3-b4) removes the stalemate, as now the rook's file is blocked.

D1 Black to move is stalemated

Especially in the ending of King + Queen versus King, beginners tend to show a 'liking' for giving stalemate, as *D2* shows. The mighty queen, who covers so many squares, can much more easily give stalemate than the rook, if she comes too close to the enemy king (*D2*).

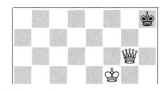

D2 The white queen gives stalemate

But the queen can also give stalemate from a distance, if she controls the only square for the enclosed king (*D3*).
What to do against stalemate? Always check if the enemy king can still play after your move – and when in doubt, just give a check!

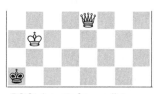

D3 Stalemate from a distance

Mate with Two Rooks

In the endgame, we can make mate with two rooks easy for ourselves: we simply put one of them somewhere on the board where it is not in the way, and give mate with the other. But that would be just like football, when a smug striker coolly dribbles in the enemy goal with the ball to his feet. As we will see, already in the middlegame there are chances to give mate with two rooks.

D1 The standard mate with 2 rooks

The principle is simple, as we can see in *D1*:
One rook closes off the penultimate (i.e. seventh or second) rank, the other gives mate on the back rank with **1.♖a6-a8#**.

Of course this does not only work on horizontal lines (ranks), but also on vertical ones (files) (*D2*), here with **1.♖f6-h6#**.
Do not get confused: the move with the other rook, *1.♖g4-h4+*, allows Black to escape for the moment.

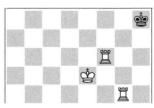

D2 Mate on the vertical lines (files)

Unlike with the mating patterns with one rook, where the enemy king must always be on the edge of the board, here we can even give mate in the middle of the board (*D3*).
The king, standing in opposition, blocks the escape forward. One rook prevents the black king's retreat, and the other gives mate.

D3 Double-rook mate in the middle

If the enemy king is caught in the corner as in *D4*, we can win with two rooks on the 7th rank.
1.♖c7-h7# wins – the ♖a7 protects its colleague.

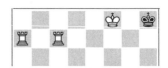

D4 Mate on the 7th rank

Things get a little more complicated if the king still has an escape square (*D5*).
But this will be of no use to him here, as now rook number 2 steps in:
1.♖c7-h7+ ♔h8-g8 2.♖a7-g7#
More mating motifs with 2 rooks will be given in the quiz on the next page.

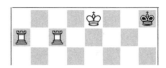

D5 Mate on the 7th rank in 2 moves

Quiz 2: Mate with Two Rooks

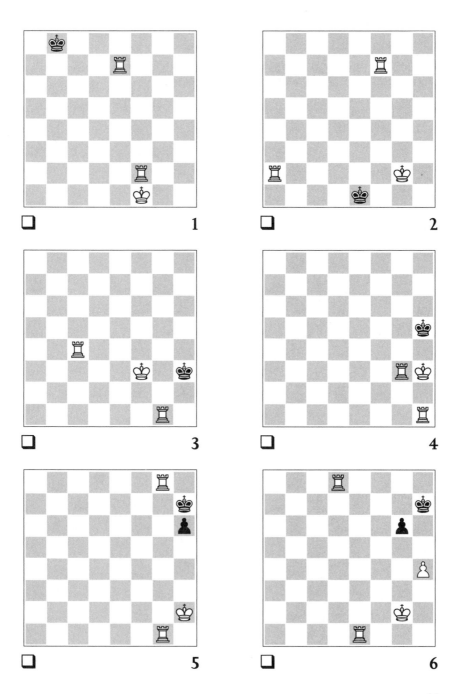

❑   **1**   ❑   **2**

❑   **3**   ❑   **4**

❑   **5**   ❑   **6**

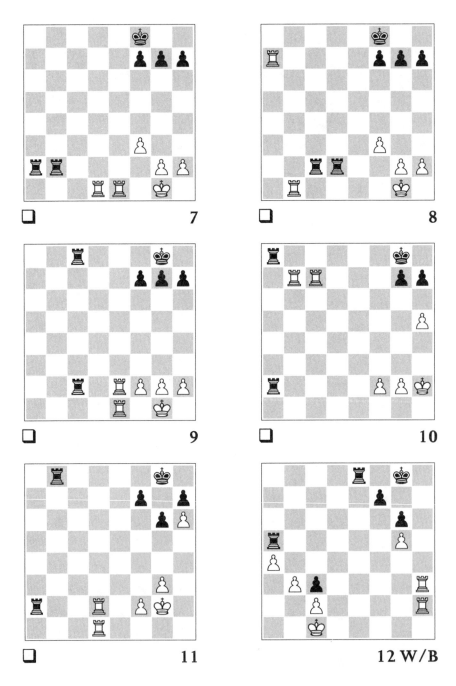

7

8

9

10

11

12 W/B

Solutions to 'Mate with Two Rooks'

1	**1.♖f2-f8#** It is not necessary for the rooks to stand close to one another, as in our model example − they can easily be standing far apart as well. The only important thing is that one rook cuts off the penultimate rank, and the other can give mate on the back rank − and, of course, none of them should get caught (i.e. captured) by the king!
2	With support from its king, the rook can also get close to the enemy king, and win by **1.♖f7-f1#**.
3	The protection zone of the white king keeps his enemy tied to the edge and this enables **1.♖g1-h1#**.
4	Who said that it always has to be a rook move that leads to mate? **1.♔h3-g2#** opens the file on which the ♖h1 operates, and thus introduces the mate!
5	The pawn on h6 is hampering the black king. White exploits this with **1.♖g1-g7#**. If you have taken the wrong rook, you will soon get a second chance to win: *1.♖g8-g7+* ♔h7-h8 2.♖g7-g8+ ♔h8-h7. Now we are again in the starting position. This time you will surely play 3.♖g1-g7#.
6	Was this exercise too difficult? Well, here things are getting yet a little more complicated. **1.♖e1-e7+** does not give mate immediately, since the king has the escape square h6. But there, he is deprived of square g5 by the white pawn, and from g6 by his own pawn. So on **1...♔h7-h6, 2.♖d8-h8#** wins.
7	We have already seen the mate on the back rank. However, with two rooks, there are even more possibilities. Here, a white rook deprives the king of the escape square e7, and the other one gives mate: **1.♖d1-d8#** [*If Black were to move*, he could play successfully on the second rank, but he could not give mate: *1...♖b2xg2+* 2.♔g1-h1 ♖g2xh2+ 3.♔h1-g1 ♖a2-g2+ 4.♔g1-f1 ♖g2-d2. Warding off the mate threat and with his two extra pawns, Black can now play for a win (*or give perpetual check by 4...♖g2-f2+ 5.♔f1-g1 ♖h2-g2+ etc.*). 5.♖d1-a1. Threatening with mate again, but giving Black time to create a *luft*: 5...g7-g6 (*or 5...♖h2-f2+ 6.♔f1-g1 ♖f2-e2, closing off the e-file*).]

8	Here, a rook on the 7th rank cuts off the escape via e7: **1.♖b1-b8+** Black can only delay the mate, but not prevent it: **1...♖c2-c8 2.♖b8xc8+ ♖d2-d8 3.♖c8xd8#**. *If Black were to move*, just as in the previous position, he could again win material. The following 'trick' is interesting: **1...♖d2xg2+ 2.♔g1-f1 ♖c2-f2+ 3.♔f1-e1 ♖g2-g1+** One rook is sacrificed in order to win the ♖b1: **4.♔e1xf2 ♖g1xb1** and White's mate threat is warded off.
9	Against two rooks on one file (**'rook doubling'**), one guard on the back rank is not enough: **1.♖e2-e8+ ♖c8xe8 2.♖e1xe8#** *If Black were to move*, he would win: **1...♖c2xe2** and White cannot capture in view of 2.♖e1xe2 ♖c8-c1+ 3.♖e2-e1 ♖c1xe1#. So there remains 2.♖e1-f1, but now with 2...♖c8-e8 Black can immediately exchange one rook, which is the simplest and safest way to win: 3.g2-g3 ♖e2-e1 4.♖f1xe1 ♖e8xe1+ 5.♔g1-g2 ♔g8-f8 and Black wins easily.
10	The white rooks have doubled on the 7th rank, which always creates a dangerous situation. **1.♖c7xg7+ ♔g8-f8** [1...♔g8-h8 does not change anything: 2.♖g7xh7+ ♔h8-g8 3.♖b7-g7+ ♔g8-f8 4.h5-h6] **2.♖g7xh7** Threatening mate on the back rank. **2...♔f8-g8 3.♖b7-g7+ ♔g8-f8 4.h5-h6** Supporting the rook and thereby enabling White, after **4...♖a2xf2** or any other move, to play **5.♖h7-h8#**. Without the possibility to protect the rook, White would still have had to show good technique to win this game.
11	The *luft* on g7 does not help the king, since it is controlled by the advanced pawn on h6, so: **1.♖d2-d8+ ♖b8xd8 2.♖d1xd8#** Such positions – when a hole on g7 can be exploited by an advanced pawn nestling on h6 or f6 – are always highly dangerous.
12	The open h-file can be used for dangerous attacks with rooks. Here White wins by **1.♖h3-h8+ ♔g8-g7 2.♖h2-h7#**. The pawn on g5 blocks the escape square f6. *If Black were to move*, he could win more easily by **1...♖e8-e1#**. Here also, the constricting pawn on c3 prevents the escape of the king.

Mate with the Queen

The queen combines the qualities of rook and bishop. She can function as a substitute for either of these pieces, which means that we can use the mating patterns by the rook we have learned, with the queen as well. So we will not show you these elementary mating patterns again – we will immediately turn to the extra possibilities of the queen.

In *D1* the queen can either give mate like a rook by **1.♕d5-d8#**, or play like a bishop with **1.♕d5-b7#** or even **1.♕d5-g8#**.

The extra bishop property is what makes the queen so dangerous. She can control more squares than the rook and thus give mate much more quickly and easily. In *D2*, a rook could not give mate immediately, as its king does not have the opposition and is not standing on b3. But this will already do for the queen: **1.♕g2-b2#**.

The same goes for *D3*: **1.♕b2-g2#** wins even without the opposition.

In *D4* the queen is standing behind the king. For the rook this would be a 'blind spot' from which it could not attack. However, the queen can do this thanks to her extra bishop property: **1.♕g5-d8#**.
Playing along a diagonal, a queen can suddenly emerge on the back rank from a great distance, and give mate from 'deep space'.

In positions with little space the queen is very dangerous due to her versatility, and she can often create surprising mates, like in *D5*: **1.♕f5-f4#**. The pawn on g2 and the ♖h3 are blocking the escape squares, the white king controls the f2-square, and with her rook property, the queen cuts off the 4th rank, whereas she gives mate with her bishop function.

D1 Mate with rook
move or bishop move

D2 Mate in the corner

D3 Mate on the penultimate rank

D4 Mate from the 'blind spot'
and from the 'deep'

D5 Mate in a constricted position

Quiz 3: Mate with the Queen

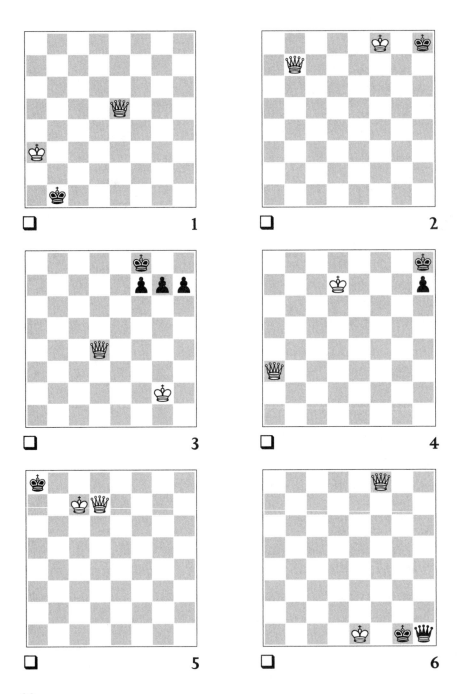

❑ 1   ❑ 2

❑ 3   ❑ 4

❑ 5   ❑ 6

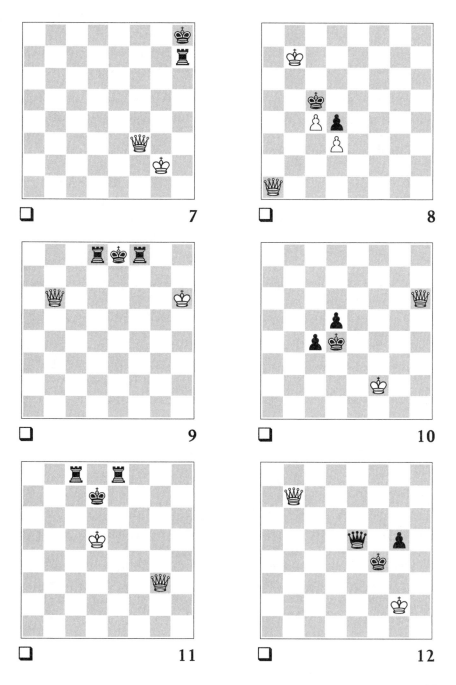

Solutions to 'Mate with the Queen'

1	1.♛e5-b2# Instead, *1.♛e5-e1+?* ♚b1-c2 allows the king to escape.
2	'So where would you like to get it, sire?' the queen asks, giving him a choice between two mates: **1.♛b7-g7#** or *1.♛b7-h1#*, a mate from the greatest possible distance.
3	**1.♛d4-d8#** With a rook the king would be able to escape, but the queen also controls his escape square e7. The queen could also give mate on d8 coming from h4 or a5.
4	The white troops are standing at a distance, but that doesn't mean that the black king is safe: **1.♛a3-f8#** The pawn on h7 prevents his flight forward. If on every turn you extend in your mind the direction of your opponent's pieces as well as your own, you will find such moves and you won't experience any nasty surprises!
5	A rook would be standing on a 'blind spot' here, but the bishop property of the queen can take her anywhere: **1.♛d7-a4#** More time-consuming is *1.♛d7-c8+/c6+* ♚a8-a7 2.♛c8/c6-b7#.
6	Both sides have a queen, and normally speaking in such cases, if no big mistakes are made, the game will end in a draw. But the black king is locked up on the right by his own queen, and on the left by his opponent – and the white queen makes use of this: **1.♛f8-f2#** This time she has approached in the way of the rook, she cuts off the f-file and the second rank like a rook, and gives mate like a bishop! This mate would also be possible if the white king were on e2, e3 or g3.
7	Yes, the queen is far away, but from the depths of space she is as quick as lightning to get to the black king, whose flight forward is obstructed by his own rook: **1.♛f3-f8#** You should always pay attention to such possibilities if there are still queens on the board in the endgame!
8	Her rook property allows the queen to reach the mating square, where she only requires her bishop function, since the black king only has the squares b4 and d6 available. And these are controlled by **1.♛a1-a3#**.

9	The king is flanked by his rooks, but this doesn't protect him against the frontal attack **1.♛b6-e6#**. This motif is called '**epaulette mate**'. The name is derived from the yokes worn on officer uniforms in former days, i.e. the epaulettes. However, they used to shine like gold, whereas the rooks are looking rather dismal here – and the king is looking quite ma(t)te!
10	Moves like **1.♛h6-e3#** here have ended many a game abruptly. This mating picture shows the full power of the queen: she cuts off the e-file and the 3rd rank like a rook, and controls the e3-a7 diagonal like a bishop. This 'diagonal mate' has already decided many games by surprise, or even completely turned certain games around!
11	We are already familiar with the 'epaulette mate'. A different version of this mate is given in this position, with a king that has inquisitively edged forward. But inquisitiveness can be bad for your health: **1.♛g3-d6#** Instead, weak would be *1.♛g3-g7+?* ♖e8-e7 and White has spoiled his winning chances – the game should now end in a draw.
12	If the king were between his pieces here, as in the epaulette mate position, everything would be fine and nothing could hurt him. But he has edged forward too light-heartedly and after **1.♛b7-f3#** his pieces block his sideways retreat. Another version of the epaulette mate, though this time not on the edge but in the middle of the board.

Now we have seen many possibilities for the strong queen, and you must surely look forward to giving mate to someone's king with your queen.

But one thing you should always remember: the strength of the queen – her control of so many squares – also has a disadvantage:

With the queen we can give stalemate much more easily than with any other piece! You have seen an example of this in *D3* of the 'Stalemate' chapter. Therefore you should always pay attention and not carelessly put your queen anywhere on the board – always keep a careful eye on the enemy king, otherwise your anticipations of victory may quickly turn to disappointment, and your opponent will be able to relish an unhoped-for half point!

Mate with the Bishop

The bishop much less often manages to give mate than, for instance, the rook. There are only few positions where this is even technically possible, and the bishop always needs the support not only of its king, but also of other pieces (enemy pieces too) that surround the king.

Why is this? Well, the bishop can only move on squares of one colour. Therefore it cannot chase the king like a rook or a queen, hunt him down and mate him. If the bishop gives check, the king can move to a square of another colour and he is safe.

D1 Corner mate with the bishop

If the enemy king is standing in the corner, then the chances for the bishop increase, as the opponent has fewer escape squares available (provided, that is, that the corner square is of the same colour as the bishop). If one of its own pawns is also standing in the way and the king is enclosed by enemy pieces, then the king can become a prey for the bishop, as *D1* shows: **1.♗g5-f6#**.

D2 Mate in the middle

However, the presence of several pieces – your own or your opponent's – can also lead to the execution of the king in the middle of the board. *D2* shows such a position. The king and the white pawns cut off four escape squares, Black's own pawn blocks another, and the final two are taken away from him by the move **1.♗h6-f8#**.

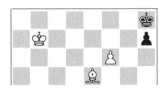

D3 Mate in the opening

Already in the opening a bishop can give mate, if the opponent does not pay attention, and especially if he does not castle in good time. This is the case in *D3*: **1.♗d3-g6#**.

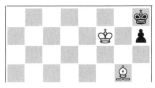

D4 Mate by discovered check

If a piece or a pawn is standing in front of the bishop and then moves away, this can also lead to mate. In *D4*, **1.f6-f7#** wins. The discovery by the pawn opens the line of the bishop and at the same time covers the escape square g8.

Mate with Two Bishops

The weakness of the bishop is that it can only attack squares of one colour. This changes significantly with two bishops. The **'bishop pair'** is very dangerous, and together with the king it can give mate. Especially when there is much open space on the board and the long diagonals are open, the bishop pair can display its full power.

D1 The typical bishops' mate in the corner

In *D1* we see a typical mate with the king in the corner. He is surrounded by the white king and the light-squared bishop, and the dark-squared bishop plays **1.♗b8-e5#**.

D2 Bishops' mate on the edge

The bishop pair with the king can only give mate on the edge of the board, but it does not necessarily have to be in the corner. *D2* shows such a mate on the edge: **1.♗c4-a6#**.
A typical mating motif – the king is caught in the crossfire of the bishops. Bad would be **1.♗c4-e6+**, when the king escapes via b7.

D3 The nailed-down king

In *D3*, the king and the dark-squared bishop have nailed the black king to the edge of the board, and the other bishop gives mate with **1.♗e2-d3#**.
Already in the opening the bishop pair can be a decisive factor. We have seen how a lone bishop can give mate to an enclosed king (*D3 on the previous page*). With two bishops these chances even improve.

D4 The bishop pair in the opening

In *D4*, the dark-squared bishop deprives the king of the squares on the a3-f8 diagonal, and at the same time prevents Black's kingside castling, which is already annoying. The square g6 is a so-called 'hole' in the position, because it is protected by neither pawns nor pieces. This is always dangerous, and here it even spells the end for Black: **1.♗d3-g6#**. The ♘d7 helps White with the mate, obstructing the escape square d7 for its king.

Quiz 4: Mate with One or Two Bishops

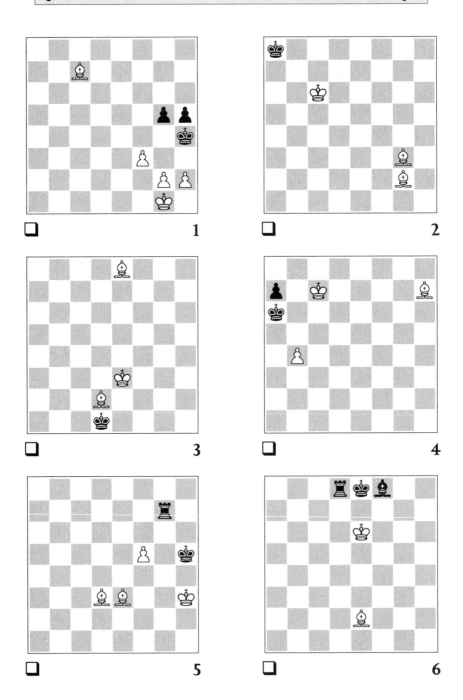

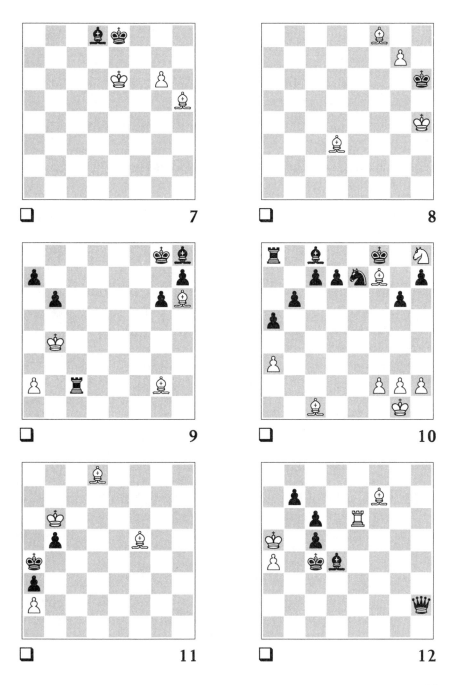

❏   7

❏   8

❏   9

❏   10

❏   11

❏   12

Solutions to 'Mate with One or Two Bishops'

1	Its own pawns block the black king's retreat. The enemy pawns deprive him of the rest of the squares. The bishop exploits this with **1.♗c7-g3#**.
2	The bishops are not always obliged to move 'personally' to enforce a mate. Here it is the white king who steps aside with **1.♔c6-b6#**, opening the diagonal for the bishop. Take care that you play the right king move, otherwise the black king would escape again!
3	The white king does not have the opposition, but that is not needed here. He deprives the black king of the escape square e2, his bishop controls c1 and e1, and **1.♗e8-a4#** takes the c2-square from him, which suffices for mate. **1.♗e8-h5+?**, however, would be weak: 1...♔d1-c2 and it will take a lot of moves before the king is again in a position to be mated.
4	The white king and his pawn control many escape squares; the last one is taken from the black king by his own a7 pawn, and so **1.♗h7-d3#** works.
5	**1.♗d3-e2+** does not give mate immediately, because the rook can post itself before the king. But actually, after **1...♖g7-g4** not much has changed. The black king's retreat is cut off by the pawn and the dark-squared bishop. After **2.♗e2xg4#** the game is over. Pieces or pawns that defend against a check by interposing, but can be captured immediately, can often be ignored during a mating attack. It is only different if, for instance, they vacate an escape square for the king or enable another piece to interfere.
6	The king is boxed in by his own pieces and has no protection against **1.♗e2-h5#**. This is similar to the epaulette mate. On the other hand, **1.♗e2-b5+** would only lead to a draw: 1...♖d8-d7 2.♗b5xd7+ ♔e8-d8 and although White could theoretically still win, his chances are very slim. Do you know the position in which Black can still be mated? Try to imagine it. You will find the answer at the end of these solutions under *S1* (S= Special questions).
7	This mating pattern you already know as the 'corner mate'. However, it is also possible anywhere on the edge of the board if the king is deprived of a square next to him, as here by his ♗d8. **1.g6-g7#** opens the diagonal for the bishop and at the same time covers the escape square f8.

8	The pawn move **1.g7-g8♕#** not only leads to promotion, but also to mate. In fact, White can promote to any piece, it is always mate! If you want to be perfectly sure, you can even promote to a knight and give two checks ('**double check**'). We will take a closer look at this concept in the next chapter.
9	The black rook attacks the pawn on a2 and the bishop on g2 at the same time. This is called a '**double attack**'. However, with **1.♗g2-d5#** the white bishop can not only escape and protect the pawn, it also conjures up a mate! The king is restricted by the dark-squared bishop, and his own people are standing in his way. Here the rook gave the bishop a good idea!
10	The white bishop, protected by its knight, takes squares e8 and g8 from the king. The black knight blocks the escape square on the left. The dark-squared bishop exploits the holes in the pawn structure with **1.♗c1-h6#**.
11	If White plays 1.♗f5-c2+ immediately, the king can escape without trouble: 1...♔a4-b4. Here the mate needs to be prepared. This can be done in two ways. Either **1.♗d8-e7 b5-b4** and **2.♗f5-d7#**, or **1.♔b6-c5** b5-b4 2.♗f5-d7#. [In both cases, the win takes a little more time after 2.♗f5-c2+: 2...b4-b3 3.♗c2xb3#] First either the king or the dark-squared bishop takes the escape square b4 away from Black. Then the mate is easy. The preparation of a mate is just as important as the mating attack itself, since we cannot count on the opponent making a grave mistake. Instead, we must always look at how we can improve the possibilities to give mate. This can be done either by involving a new piece in the battle, by cutting off a line, or by further enclosing the king.
12	Materially Black is better — only his king has ventured a little too forward. White can exploit this by clearing the bishop diagonal by a discovered check with the rook, at the same time cutting off the 3rd rank for the black king: **1.♖e6-e3#** [1.♖e6-e2+ would allow the king to escape, but it would at least win the queen.] A '**discovered check**' is a dangerous weapon, because it allows the position to be changed in two ways with one move (the bishop works along the diagonal, the rook cuts off the 3rd rank). Moreover, because of the check, the possibilities for the defender are severely limited — after all, he has to take care of his king first.

S1 White can only win if the black king goes to a light corner square (a8 or h1) and moves his bishop before or next to him. On the left a possible mating position is given. Here is another position: White: ♔c7, Black: ♔a8, ♗a7 and again mate on the long diagonal. But White cannot force these positions.

Double Check

Sometimes you wish you could play two moves at a time, as then the win would be in your pocket. Of course, that is not possible, but in certain situations it almost is: when you can give a double check.

A double check means that two pieces give check at the same time. This can only be done with a discovered check: one piece gives check and at the same time clears the way for another piece, which now also gives check. The only way the opponent can defend against a double check is by moving his king.

D1 White plays and wins immediately

In *D1*, White can win by both **1.♘e4xf6#** and **1.♘e4-d6#**. Black could easily defend himself against either the queen check or the knight check – but not against both of them at the same time!

In *D2*, the white rook is hanging. But thanks to the double check **1.♘e8-f6#** this is not a problem. The knight not only gives the necessary second check – it also deprives the black king of the escape square h7 at the same time, and this is what actually makes the mate possible.

D2 White plays and wins immediately

In *D3* everything is not finished right away, but still the double check **1.♗d2-g5+** leads to victory. **1...♚d8-c7** is met by **2.♗g5-d8#**. If Black plays *1...♚d8-e8*, then 2.♖d1-d8# wins.

Do you already fancy winning a few positions with double checks? On the next page you can find our quiz on this subject.

D3 White plays and gives mate in 2 moves

Quiz 5: Double Check Wins at Once!

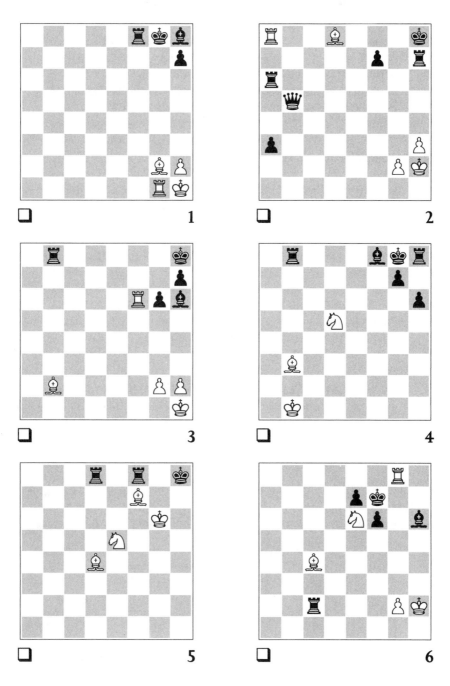

Solutions to 'Double Check Wins at Once!'

1	Rook and bishop attack the boxed-in king with **1.♗g2-d5#**.
2	What we have seen the knight do in *D2* in the explanation part, also works with the bishop. True, it cannot control the escape square h7, but here the black rook takes over this task: **1.♗d8-f6#**.
3	If you bravely employ the double check **1.♖f6-f8#** here, you will be immediately rewarded with victory. It will take longer if you have only seen **1.♖f6-b6+**. This is only a discovery with a check and an attack on the rook, though it does win: 1...♔h8-g8 2.♖b6xb8+ (1...♗h6-g7? 2.♖b6xb8#). Of course, **1.♖f6xg6+??** ♖b8xb2 would be very bad. White loses, because after 2.♖g6xh6 there follows 2...♖b2-b1#. Therefore, White cannot take the bishop. He has lost a piece and due to Black's mate threat he will lose his rook as well.
4	**1.♘d5-f6#** fires off two checks and closes off the escape square for the king! The bishop cannot move at all, as then its king would be in check, but that is not a problem. Even a piece that cannot move may give mate!
5	Okay, we have been cheating a little here – in this position a double check is not even possible. But you should also be alert, not believe everything and, of course, find the right way to win. The black king is already in a mating position, and the discovery **1.♘e5-d7#** not only opens the bishop's diagonal with check, it also protects the bishop from the attack by the ♖d8.
6	Here White even has two equivalent possibilities: **1.♘e6-g5#** or **1.♘e6-d8#**. The bishop gives check and at the same time protects the rook, which cuts off the king's escape both backwards and to the right – otherwise the mate would not be possible.

Mate with One or Two Knights

For a novice player, the knight is the trickiest piece, but when it comes to giving mate it is the weakest piece of all. It cannot even force mate together with the king and a second knight – it needs still more support. Only if the king is hampered by its own or an enemy piece, can the knight strike.

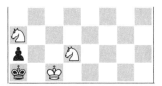

D1 The knight gives mate

In *D1*, either of the two knights can give mate on its own. Both **1.♘a3-c2#** and **1.♘d2-b3#** win. But without the pawn on a2, the king would run away.

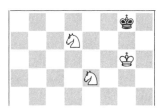

D2 Mate with the knight pair – or is it?

In *D2* White's position is optimal: the king in opposition, the knight is ready to attack. But it is not enough if Black does not cooperate: **1.♘d7-f6+ ♚g8-h8??** [With 1...♚g8-f8 the king can get away, e.g. 2.♘e5-d7+ ♚f8-e7] **2.♘e5-f7#**. This is the only mating position that is possible with a Knight Pair together with a King.

But if the opponent is deprived of even one square only, as by the pawn on b7 in *D3*, then a knight pair can reach great heights and can even win without help of the king: **1.♘d7-b6#**.

D3 Mate with the help of an enemy pawn

In confined positions, the knight is a true hero. It can jump over a massive wall of defenders and present the king with a devastating check! In *D4* the king's position is massively defended, but that does not help one bit against **1.♘d6-f7#**. Such a mate, where the king is surrounded by his own pieces, is also called '**Smothered Mate**'.

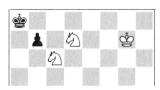

D4 Smothered Mate

In *D5*, one knight is locking up the king, and the other finishes the job by **1.♘d6-f7#**.
But the knight is strongest when it cooperates with other pieces!

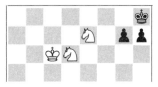

D5 Mate in the corner

41

Quiz 6: Mate with One or Two Knights

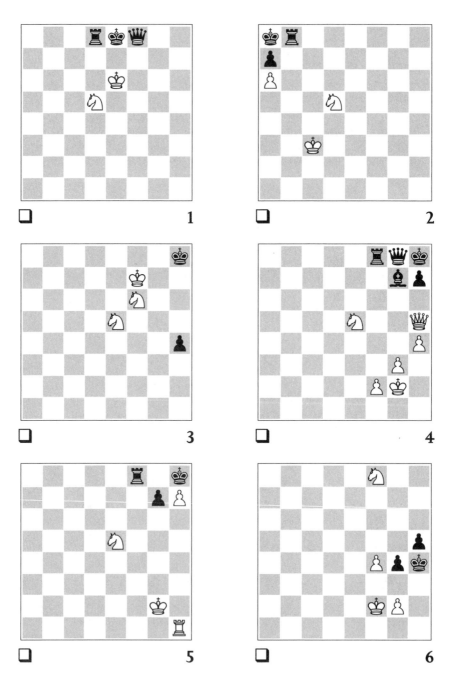

1

2

3

4

5

6

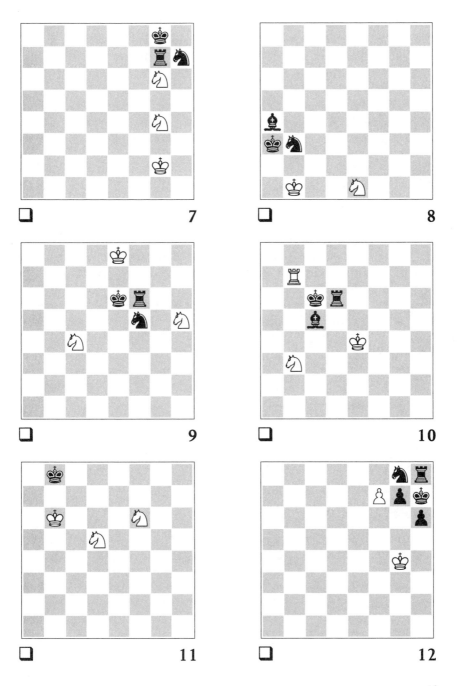

❑ 7

❑ 8

❑ 9

❑ 10

❑ 11

❑ 12

Solutions to 'Mate with One or Two Knights'

1	The king's strongest officers are at his side – and, unfortunately, also in his way, which ensures victory for White against the superior army of the enemy: **1.♘d5-c7#**.
2	The white pawn, which has marched forward, is cramping Black's king, and the latter's own rook is doing the same. Thus, the knight can easily catch the cornered king with **1.♘d5-c7#**. A pawn on c6 instead of a6 would also create a mating position.
3	In the ending with King + Two Knights versus King, it is not good for the weaker side to have a pawn. As this pawn temporarily prevents stalemate, the side with the knights can reach a winning position, which would not be possible otherwise. This last pawn does not even have to stand in the way of its king – it is already threatening him by its pure existence! Here White reaches a mating position by **1.♘e5-g6#**.
4	The pawn on h7 would normally defend the g6-square. But since the white queen is on the h-file, the pawn cannot defend anything, for if it would capture something on g6, its king would be in check and that cannot be. We call this a '**pin**' (more on this subject on page 58, 'The Pin'). This allows the move **1.♘e5-g6#**, which again creates a Smothered Mate.
5	Annoyingly for White, his own pawn on h7 is the best protection for the enemy king against the ♖h1. However, fortunately he has a knight, which reaches over the heads of friend and foe: **1.♘e5-g6#**. Precisely in such positions, where it is hard to approach your opponent, the knight often serves as the 'great executioner'.
6	The black king's retreat is barred by the f4 pawn, which controls the escape square g5. And in front of him, the white king and the g2 pawn block the way. And then of course his own pawns are hampering him as well. Such positions are ideal for an attack with the knight: **1.♘f8-g6#**. By the way, on f5 a knight would also give mate.

7	Materially speaking, Black is better, and he would soon win a knight if White focused on defence, e.g.: *1.♘g4-e5 ♘h7-f8 2.♔g2-f3 ♘f8xg6* etc. But as so often, attack is the best – and the only correct – defence. White exploits the constricted position of the black king to create a typical Two-Knights Mate: **1.♘g4-h6#**.
8	A knight can control two connected squares (here, a3 and b4). This property enables it to give check on one square and block the other (escape) square. If there are a few other pieces in the way as well, then the enemy king is done for: **1.♘e1-c2#**.
9	If several pieces are standing in the way, a Two-Knights Mate is also possible in the middle of the board: **1.♘h5-f4#**.
10	The aforementioned ability of the knight to control two neighbouring squares allows White to win in this position too. The attacked white rook, which cuts off the black king from the 7th rank, does not have to budge, since after **1.♘b3-a5#** it is protected by the knight, which gives check at the same time. And without an escape square this means immediate mate, of course. But how could this position have come about? We can imagine that the king was in check on d7, and his last move was ♔d7-c6, walking right into the mate. ♔d7-e6 would have avoided this and then the game would probably have ended in a draw. This shows how important it is to recognize possible mating patterns in time!
11	Hopefully you have realized in time that Two Knights + King cannot force the win. You might dream of **1.♘f6-d7+ ♔b8-a8??** (simply 1...♔b8-c8 averts the danger) **2.♘d5-c7#**. But you can never count on this, because any opponent will spot this mate. Besides, as a rule no-one should ever move his king into the corner if it isn't strictly necessary – that is almost never a good idea.
12	In an unusual way, the knight forces the win here. 'Which knight?' you might well ask. At the moment there is only a pawn on the board, but it moves to the promotion square with **1.f7-f8♘#**, promoting not to a queen but to a knight, which at once gives check and mate to the enclosed king. If a pawn is promoted to a lesser piece than the queen, we call this an **'underpromotion'**. This can be very useful now and then, in order to avoid stalemate, e.g. by choosing a rook instead of a queen.

Mate with (a) Pawn(s)

True, the pawn is the weakest piece on the board, but mate is mate, no matter who gives it. Certainly, the pawn also needs support – at least by one colleague pawn and its king, as in *D1*, where **1.d6-d7#** wins, since both pawns take all the back rank squares away from the black king and the latter cannot retreat. Such mating positions are only possible at the edge of the board.

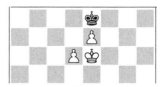

D1 King on the edge

If there are enemy pieces taking away squares from their king, there are many chances to give mate. In *D2* the black a7 pawn shuts the door on the escape route for its own king, and **1.b6-b7#** decides.

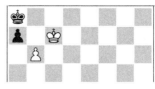

D2 Own pawn blocks the way

In *D3* Black has an overwhelming advantage in a material sense, but the king's right side is undefended, and so **1.f6-f7#** wins. His own pieces are boxing in their king.

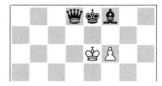

D3 Epaulette mate with a pawn

In *D4* the black king is cut off from the edge of the board by the rook. Thus, there is no escape for the king after **1.g5-g6#**.

No king should venture onto the battlefield in front of its pieces. In *D5*, Black's recklessness is immediately punished by either **1.f2-f3#** or **1.h2-h3#**.

D4 Cutting off from behind

One mating possibility which is only available to the pawn, we have seen already in the Knight quiz, Exercise 12: promotion. A pawn can promote and directly give mate.

However, outside the endgame the pawn does not have great chances to give mate. Its strength lies more in the possibility to take away squares, to surround the king, or to support other pieces, which force the actual mate.

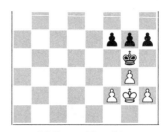

D5 The reckless king

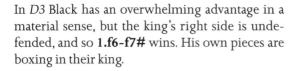

Quiz 7: Mate with (a) Pawn(s)

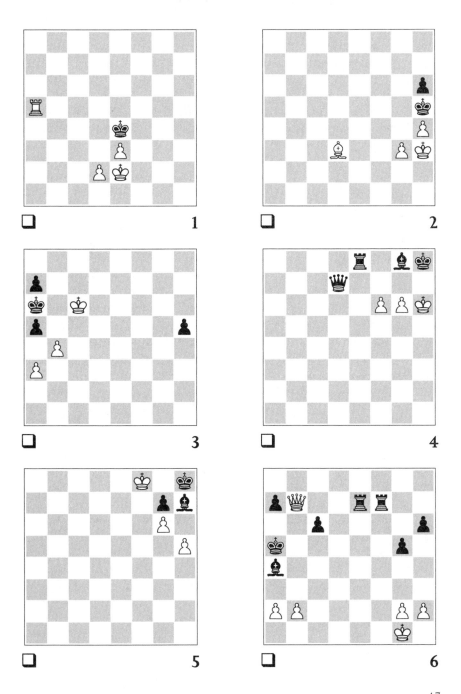

❑ 1

❑ 2

❑ 3

❑ 4

❑ 5

❑ 6

Solutions to
'Mate with (a) Pawn(s)'

1	If the enemy king's retreat is cut off by a queen or rook, pawns can also give mate in the middle of the board – not only at the edge: **1.d2-d3#**.
2	The situation is similar if a bishop controls the diagonal on which the escape square of the king lies: **1.g3-g4#**. If the bishop is far away or if the position is complex, then this possibility is often overlooked by beginners.
3	The boxed-in black king is helpless against **1.b4-b5#**. Precisely in closed positions at the edge of the board, a pawn can often give mate.
4	Here the first pawn cannot achieve the aim, since it can be stopped by the queen. But no. 2 manages to give the mate: **1.g6-g7+ ♛d7xg7+ 2.f6xg7#**
5	Here a pawn march or a pawn break must be forced on the g-file. **1.h5-h6** [1.g6xh7? leads to a draw: 1...♚h8xh7 2.♚f8-f7 ♚h7-h6 3.♚f7-g8 ♚h6xh5 4.♚g8xg7] **1...g7xh6 2.g6-g7#** This line is not forced, as Black can also play *1...♗h7xg6*. But now 2.h6xg7+ ♚h8-h7 3.g7-g8♛+ wins, as White will eventually be able to force the mate.
6	Do you see Black's threat? The threat is ♖e7-e1#, and since the attacked queen cannot prevent this, she seems lost. But this is not at all relevant, since a brave pawn helps her out of this fix with **1.b2-b4#**. A two-square march with the pawn from its first rank can also force mate.

Exercise
'Placing the king to give mate'

In this exercise you are required to find the square on which the king has to be in order for White to be able to give mate. With a little concentration and knowledge of the mating patterns we have learned, you will manage this!

Tip: sometimes more than one square is possible! Solutions on the next page.

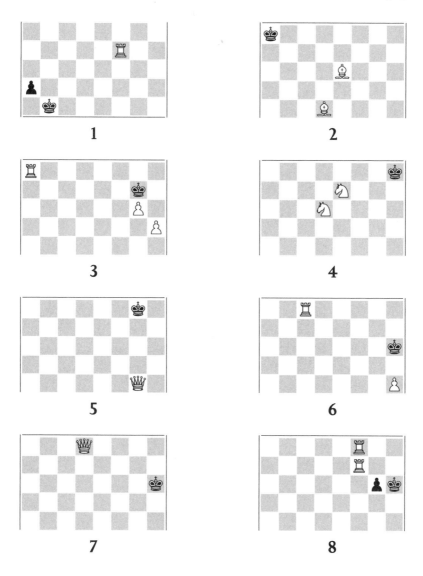

1

2

3

4

5

6

7

8

Solutions 'Placing the king to give mate'

1	♔b3/♔c3	♖f4–f1#	5	♔g6	♕g4–c8#
2	♔c7/♔c8	♗e6–d5#	6	♔f7/♔f6	♖c8–h8#
3	♔g5	h5–h6#	7	♔f7/♔f6/♔f5	♕c8–h4#/h8#
4	♔g6/♔h6	♘d6–f7#	8	♔f4/♔f6/♔g4/♔h4	♖f8–h8#

Part II
Mating Patterns with Several Pieces and/or in More than One Move

In Part I we have dealt with the way the individual pieces work. Granted, now and then an enemy piece was helping with the mate, and sometimes other pieces joined in to help catch their own king, but it was largely the pieces concerned that were 'qualified' to give the mate. However, in practice it happens far more often that several different pieces contribute to the mate. Examples of such 'teamwork' are a mate with Rook + Bishop or Knight, or with Two Bishops and one Pawn, and there are many other possibilities. Also, enemy pawns or pieces which, for instance, block escape squares for their king, can help decide the game. In this chapter we will deal with the most important mating patterns with several pieces, and learn how the individual pieces can cooperate optimally.

Unfortunately, these positions cannot be so easily comprehended and systematized as in the exercises with single pieces + King. It is inherent in the multi-sidedness of the game of chess that, as soon as there are more pieces involved, the number of possibilities and positions explodes. In fact, this is not so tragic. Nobody could quickly learn all the possible mating patterns by heart anyway. Only with the passing of time and with growing practical experience will you get a firm feel for tactical possibilities.

If in the following quizzes you are not able to solve some of the exercises, this is no problem at all. The aim is to learn, not to solve as many exercises as possible. The exercises presented next are substantially more difficult than those in Part I. Do not be sad and do not get discouraged if there are several solutions you do not manage to find – take a look at the solutions and try to keep the idea in mind for the next time – or for practical games!

And now, look forward to seeing many interesting mating positions!

Mate with Rook + Knight

Rook + Knight can give mate to the enemy king in a corner without further support.

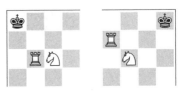

D1 Two instances of the 'Arab Mate'

In *D1*, on the *left* this can be done with **1.♖b6-b8#**, on the *right* with **1.♖e7-h7#**. So, the rook can give mate vertically as well as horizontally. We have already learned that the knight can attack two squares. Here these are the two escape squares of the king, and on one of them the rook – protected by the knight – gives mate.

About five hundred years ago, the game of chess came from the Arabic countries to Europe, and there it received many new rules. Only the way the rook and the knight moved remained unchanged, and that is why this mate has been called the '**Arab Mate**'. The Arab Mate can also occur in various forms.

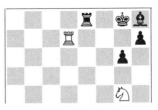

D2 'Arab Variant'

In *D2*, White is helped by the black pieces, who are boxing in their king: **1.♘g4-h6+ ♚g8-f8 2.♖d7-f7#**.

If the bishop were on f8 instead of h8, the normal mating pattern would be introduced by **1.♘g4-f6+**.

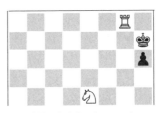

D3 The knight gives mate

It doesn't always have to be the rook that gives mate. In *D3* the knight takes over this task with **1.♘e4-f6#**, protecting the rook at the same time.

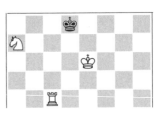

D4 The knight covers the mating square

In *D4*, the knight only controls the mating square c8, the king holds off his counterpart, and the rook completes the picture with **1.♖c4-c8#**.

But the knight can also perfectly well perform the task of controlling the escape squares of the king.

D5 The knight blocks the exit

In *D5* it cuts off both the boltholes on a7 and c7, and the rook executes the mate with **1.♖g6-g8#**.

Even from 'unsuspected positions' the knight can cut off the escape from the king, as shown in *D6*:
1.♖d6-d8#.
A knight on c6, d5 or f5 would also cut off the escape square e7.

D6 Knight cuts off
the escape square

In *D7* the situation is similar. The rook controls the open file and the knight blocks the escape square g8.

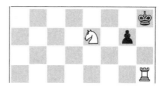

D7 Mate on the open h-file

If his own pieces are in his way, the king can be caught by the Rook + Knight, not only in the corner or on the edge of the board, but practically anywhere. *D8* shows an example of how an advanced king is cut off to the side by the knight and by one of its own pawns.
Even more possibilities occur if the rook or the knight is protected by a pawn.

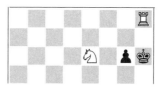

D8 Knight cuts off the
advanced king

In *D9* we see how an advanced pawn contributes to the mate. In the sub-diagram on the *left* it protects only the knight and thus enables an Arab Mate (with the help of the black g7 pawn) – instead, on the *right*, it also cuts off the escape square e6 for the king, thus contributing actively to the mate.
Such support can also be provided by the king or by another piece.

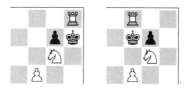

D9 Mate with the help of a
supporting pawn

In *D10*, the white king supports the rook on the mating square e7. His place could also be taken by a bishop (i.e. on one of the diagonals which include the square e7), or a pawn on d6 or f6, or another knight on c6/d5/f5/g6...

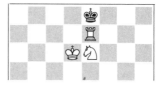

D10 Mate with support by the king

The number of possibilities increases immensely as more pieces are involved, either your own or your enemy's.

Quiz 8: Mate with Rook + Knight

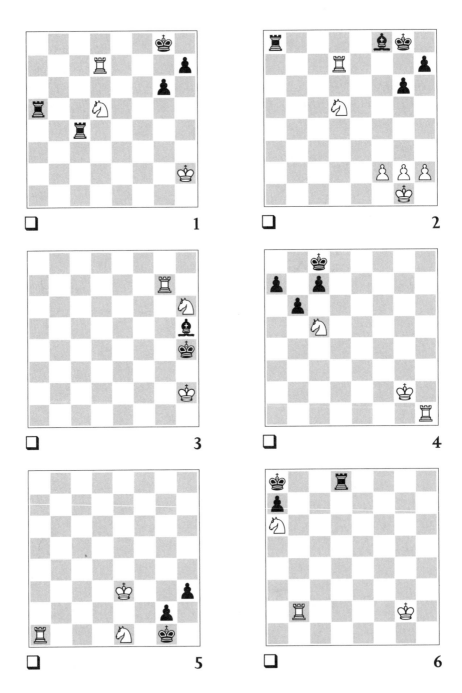

❑   1   ❑   2

❑   3   ❑   4

❑   5   ❑   6

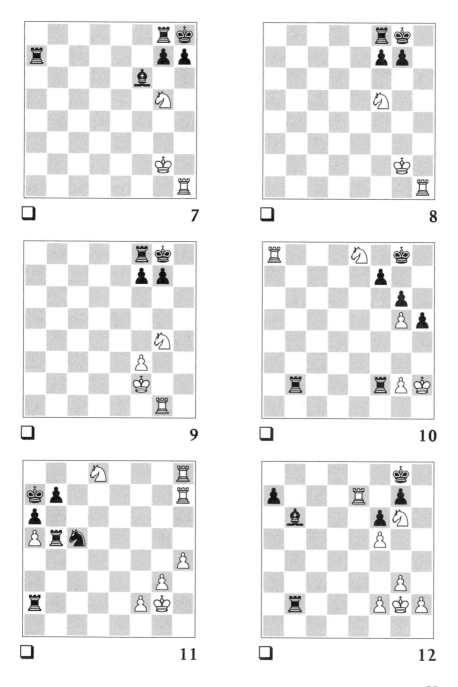

Solutions to 'Mate with Rook + Knight'

1	Here the Arab Mate isn't possible, since the king can escape to f8. But White can secure the draw: **1.♘d5-f6+ ♔g8-f8 2.♘f6xh7+ ♔f8-g8 3.♘h7-f6+ ♔g8-f8** [3...♔g8-h8?? 4.♖d7-h7#] **4.♘f6-h7+ ♔f8-e8 5.♘h7-f6+**. The knight protects the rook and gives perpetual check.
2	The bishop on f8 makes a lot of difference with the previous position. Bad luck for Black, as now **1.♘d5-f6+ ♔g8-h8 2.♖d7xh7#** does work: the Arab Mate!
3	The knight can be more than just a supporter of its rook. Here the white king blocks the way for his counterpart from the front, the rook controls the g-file, and the knight triumphs with **1.♘h6-f5#**.
4	The knight has blocked both escape squares, and thus **1.♖h1-h8#** wins.
5	Sometimes Rook + Knight can both give check and mate. This is the case here with **1.♘e1-f3#**, a discovery by the knight with double check. However, the knight is also playing an important part in the mate, as it controls the escape square h2!
6	The black rook prevents mate on b8. But it does not prevent **1.♘a6-c7#**.
7	This time the ♖a7 prevents the threatened Smothered Mate on f7. But along the h-file White can achieve mate quite easily: **1.♖h1xh7#**. The black rook blocks the way for its king's escape to the side.
8	Also here, the white rook on the open file proves fatal for the second player. However, this time it only controls the escape squares, enabling the knight to do the job: **1.♘f5-e7#**.
9	The pawn on g7 is pinned after **1.♘g4-f6+**. Therefore Black has no better than **1...♔g8-h8**, when the rook can go **2.♖g1-h1#**.
10	A double check introduces an Arab Mate. This is made possible by the support of the g5 pawn, which both protects the knight and blocks the escape square h6: **1.♘e8-f6+ ♔g8-g7 2.♖a8-g8#**.

11	This time we even have two rooks, each of which fulfils part of the task. After **1.♘d8-c6#**, one of them cuts off the 8th rank while the other pins the b7 pawn, so the knight cannot be taken. This solution is really hard to find if you don't know the trick!
12	Since the knight is protected, it can support the rook in the mating attack: **1.♖e7-e8+ ♔g8-f7 2.♖e8-f8#**, or **1...♔g8-h7 2.♖e8-h8#**.

The Pin

Sometimes you cannot move a piece or a pawn because then the king would be in check. *D1 left* shows such a case – the bishop cannot move at all. This situation is called a **'pin'**.

There are various types of pin. In *D1 middle*, the queen is pinned. However, unlike the bishop, she can still play, if only on the d6-d1 file. Thus, she can also capture her attacker.

In *D1 right*, this time the queen is involved instead of the king. This changes things slightly, for now the bishop can move, even though then the queen will be lost. By stepping aside, the bishop can either protect the queen (from f6 or h6), or it could attack another piece on another part of the board. This type of pin, which is also called a **'relative pin'**, is much more complicated than the absolute pin, which allows no moves, or only very specific ones. Most of the pins only win material. However, here we only want to deal with pins that lead directly to mate.

D1 Pins along files

Of course, pins are not limited to the vertical direction (the files). They also occur in the horizontal direction (i.e. on the ranks) and diagonally. *D2* shows us a few examples. The white rook pins the bishop, the white bishop pins the knight. Both black pieces cannot move at all. The black queen pins the pawn on g2, which enables Black, if it is his move, to play **1...♖e3-h3#**.

D2 Pins along ranks or diagonals

Quiz 9: The Pin

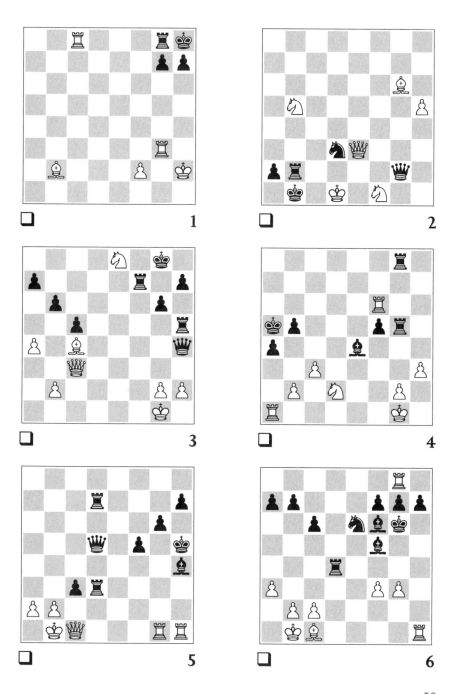

Solutions to 'The Pin'

1	White can play **1 ♗b2xg7#** unpunished, since the black rook is pinned and cannot leave the 8th rank.
2	The knight, which is pinned by the bishop, cannot protect the mating square: **1.♕e3-c1#** *A pinned piece protects nothing and nobody!*
3	Black threatens mate on the next move. But the ♖f7 is pinned by the bishop and cannot cover the mating square g7. Therefore: **1.♕c3-g7#**.
4	This position offers two mating possibilities at once: **1.♘d2-b3#** and **1.b2-b4#**. Both mates are made possible by the pin on the a4 pawn, which can neither capture the knight 'normally', nor the pawn '**en passant**' (see the explanation below).
5	The pinned ♗h4 cannot protect the g5-square, therefore: **1.♕c1-g5#**.
6	The solution to Exercise 6 is similar, but even harder to see. The g7 pawn is pinned, and so the h6-square is protected only by the king. But the latter cannot capture into check, therefore White mates with **1.♖h1-h6#**!

Capturing 'en passant'

Since most beginners and hobby players do not know this special rule, we will have a closer look at it – just in case.

En passant (pronounced 'on passon') is a French term meaning '**capturing in passing**'. It is a kind of offside rule in chess, which serves to prevent pawn formations 'freezing' too quickly. An example:

White moves the b-pawn two squares from its starting position, i.e. **1.b2-b4**. But the en passant rule assesses this pawn move as if White had only played **1.b2-b3**.

Black now has a choice: he can either leave the pawn be on b4 or capture it. In the latter case, he removes the white b-pawn and puts his own a-pawn on b3.

Capturing en passant is only possible if the pawn has moved from its starting position, and it has to be done immediately. So you cannot wait until the next move and then capture en passant: it's now or never!

Mate with Rook + Bishop

The short-paced knight should always be near the battle scene, but the bishop can also interfere from a great distance. Of course, it can operate in small spaces too – pinning, enclosing, taking away squares, protecting a rook, etc. Especially in the fight against a castled king's position, the bishop is an indispensable helper with many winning techniques at its disposal.

One of its easiest tasks is to block an escape square for the enemy king, as is shown in *D1*. There follows **1.♖c7-c8#**.

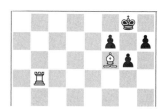

D1 Blocking the escape

In *D2*, the bishop also takes away two squares from the king. A third square (h7) remains available. However, this is of no use to the king, since after **1.♖c5-c8+ ♚g8-h7** the bishop helps the rook to play **2.♖c8-h8#**. This is one of the typical mating positions with rook and bishop.

D2 Mate in the corner

Another typical motif is shown in *D3*: the bishop standing on f6 constricts the king, and, by standing in the way of the f7 pawn ('**blockading**' it), it also makes it hard for Black to free himself from this predicament – and so it creates the conditions for the back-rank mate **1.♖b5-b8#**.

D3 The constricting bishop

In *D4*, the bishop is 'only' on h6, but this is already sufficient for mate after **1.♖d6-d8#**.
Positions *D2-D4* have in common that in all of them the hole on g7 is exploited, and because Black does not control the squares f6 and h6, the bishop can be fixed there (although *D2* shows that this is not always necessary). That is why you should think carefully before playing g7-g6, and not play it when it is not necessary, as long as the opponent has a bishop or a queen on the board.

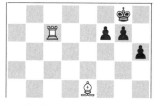

D4 The bishop on h6

Quiz 10: Mate with Rook + Bishop

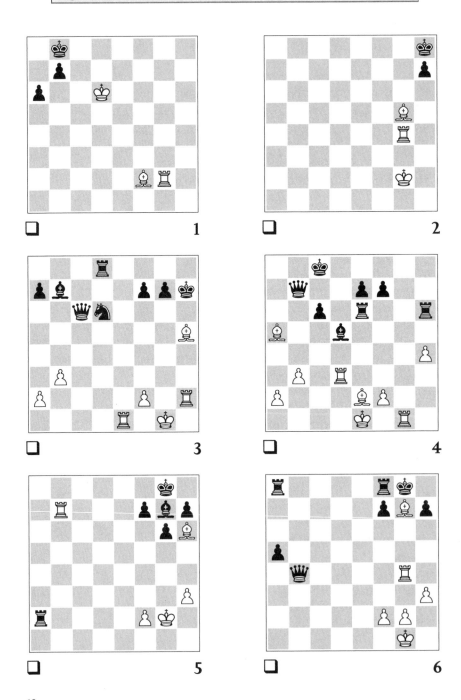

❑   1   ❑   2

❑   3   ❑   4

❑   5   ❑   6

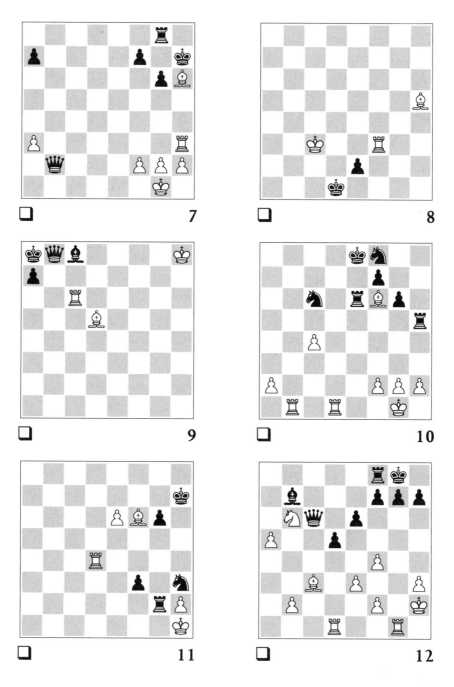

7

8

9

10

11

12

Solutions to
'Mate with Rook + Bishop'

1	So far and yet so near: not only beginners often overlook that a bishop can also control an escape square from a distance: **1.♗g2-g8#**.
2	With **1.♗g5-f6#** White not only gives check, he also vacates the g-file for the rook – and the latter cuts off the king!
3	If White can withstand the temptation to play *1.♗h5-f3+*, winning the queen, and instead deprives the king of his escape squares by **1.♗h5xf7#**, the game ends immediately!
4	**1.♖g1-g8+** is obvious, but then after **1...♔c8-d7** you must also have seen **2.♖g8-d8#**. This mating motif with Rook + Bishop is not restricted to king positions in the corner or on the edge – in a constricted position it may be possible anywhere on the board.
5	Against the **1.♖b7-b8+** check Black can defend with **1...♗g7-f8**, but this only delays the mate: **2.♖b8xf8#**.
6	**1.♗g7-d4#**. A discovery, which opens the rook file and blocks the way for the queen to the rook at the same time. Hopefully none of you have played the schematic *1.♗g7-f6+??*, as then Black can save himself by 1...♕b4xg4 and even wins!
7	White has two possibilities: the lucrative discovered check **1.♗h6-c1+**, which wins the queen after 1...♔h7-g7 2.♗c1xb2+, or the short, not very spectacular-looking move **1.♗h6-f8#**, which ends the game immediately. The discovering bishop deprives the king of the flight square g7.
8	With **1.♖f3-e3** White could conquer the passed pawn and win in a few moves (though he should always watch out for stalemate!). However, the quickest road to victory is **1.♖f3-f1#**, exploiting the pin on the e2 pawn. ***Extra question:*** What would change if, instead of the pawn, there would be a rook or a queen on e2? (*Solution below under E1*)

9	After **1.♗c6xc8#** the diagonal is opened – and so the bishop gives check – and this time the rook pins the queen, who therefore cannot move to b7.
10	The mating motif is simple and easy to see, but there is a problem. The knight protects the mate square d8 and cannot be driven off. But it also protects the mate square b8 and this means that it is overloaded with two tasks. Thus, **1.♖b1-b8+** diverts the knight from the protection of d8 and after **1...♘c6xb8, 2.♖d1-d8#** mates. If a piece is tied to two tasks (as here the knight to the protection of both the b8- and the d8-square) and can only fulfil one of these tasks at a time, we call this '**overloading**' or '**overburdening**'. It is a tactical motif in its own right, which may support or enable other mating patterns.
11	The king does not always have to be caged in by his own pawns, as in our previous illustrative examples. Here he would have free squares to escape to, if only the white e6 pawn weren't there. This chance circumstance enables White to win by **1.♖d4-h4+ ♚h7-g8 2.♖h4-h8#**. Bad luck for Black – if it were his move, he would have had a pleasant choice between 1...♖g2-g1# and 1...♘h3-f2#
12	**1.♖g1xg7+ ♚g8-h8**. Thus far we know the road to mate. But this time, 2.♖g7-g6+ is insufficient in view of 2...f7-f6. The double check **2.♖g7-g8++** does lead to success. Black can simply capture the rook, but after **2...♚h8xg8**, instead of the bishop, the rook can give check and mate, as Black cannot oppose or interpose anything! **3.♖d1-g1#**.
E1	A short answer for both pieces: **nothing**. It does not matter which piece is pinned, rook or queen, none of them can capture the white rook or move to e1.

Pieces?

The 'puppets' (as they are called by one of our young chess friends) on the chess-board are called '**pieces**'. Does this include the pawns?

In everyday usage, all the figures on the board are called 'pieces', but actually this is not entirely correct. 'Pieces' is the name for only the 'officers' (♔, ♕, ♖, ♗, ♘), not the pawns. So if someone announces that he will start a furious attack on your king with all his pieces, you might assume that he only intends to attack with his 'officers'. But he might also mean to include the pawns.

Well, you shouldn't let this worry you – you can simply speak of 'pieces' and include the pawns. The correct meaning has its significance for experts on the chess rules, who also speak of 'light' and 'dark' pieces instead of black and white ones, so as to include the possibility of brown, red or blue pieces.

The most important thing is that these pieces speak for themselves on the board – and the best thing they can say is: 'Check and Mate'!

Mate with Queen + Rook

Anything Two Rooks or Rook + Bishop can do, Queen + Rook can do as well, and much more and better!

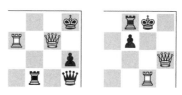
D1 The queen as a 'spearhead'

D1 illustrates this quite clearly. Two rooks would achieve nothing here, but the queen as a 'spearhead of the attack' wins easily by **1.♕h5-h7#**.
Something similar applies in the *right sub-diagram*: **1.♕h5-h8#**. Against two rooks, the king would slip away via g7 and f6.

D2

Whether horizontally or vertically, the queen only has to touch the king and the job is already done, as *D2 left* shows.
An open h-file can already mean a lethal attack if a queen doubles on it with (a) rook(s). If two files are open, the chances of a rook and queen giving mate are great, as is illustrated in *D2 right*.

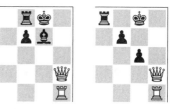
D3 Mate on the back rank

The most frequent attack by Queen + Rook is on the back rank, as shown in *D3*: **1.♕d6-d8+ ♖b8xd8 2.♖d5xd8#**.

D4 'Sidestepping the defence'

Such attacks can occur in many forms. In *D4*, White sidesteps the defender with **1.♕e5-e8+ ♖c8xe8 2.♖a8xe8#**.

D5 Decoy into mate position

In *D5*, the queen sacrifice **1.♕d6xf8+** forces the king into a mate position, and after **1...♔g8xf8** the rook rounds off the attack with **2.♖c5-c8#**.
As most of the time there will be other pieces in play – your own as well as your opponent's – the possibilities for mating attacks with Queen + Rook are great. More on this in the following quiz exercises.

Quiz 11: Mate with Queen + Rook

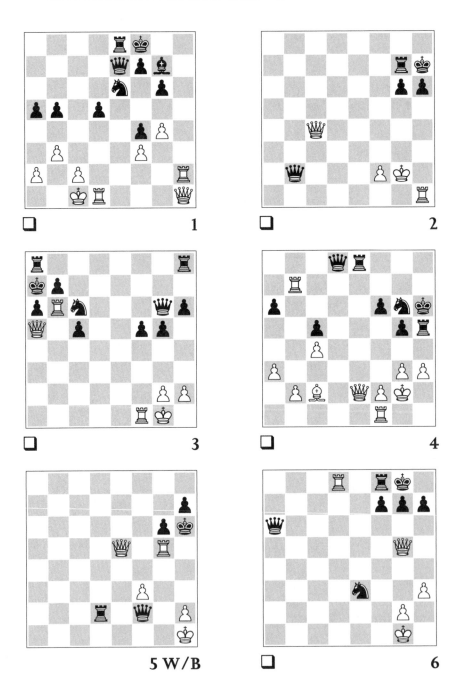

❏   1

❏   2

❏   3

❏   4

5 W/B

❏   6

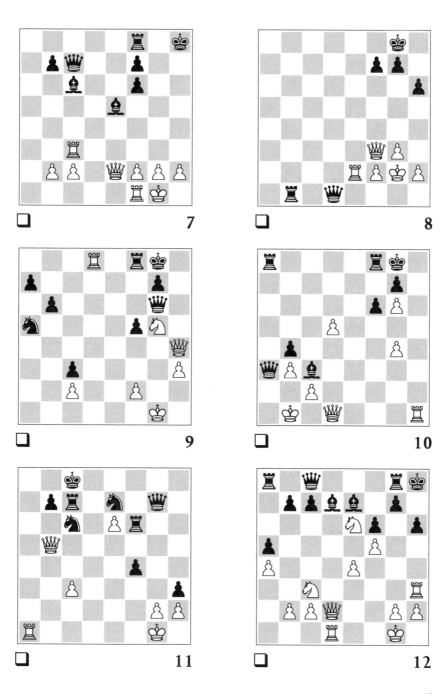

Solutions to
'Mate with Queen + Rook'

1	The black king is on f8 instead of g8 and is closely surrounded by his own pieces, so White succeeds in clearing a square for his queen with the sacrifice **1.♖h2-h8+ ♗g8xh8 2.♕h1xh8#**.
2	The rook assists its queen with the winning line clearance **1.♖h1xh6+**, because after **1...♔h7xh6** the king is stuck on the edge and helpless against **2.♕c4-h4#**.
3	White does not appear to be able to make progress here, and Black can easily defend against reinforcements like 1.♖f1-b1 by bringing up new defenders. However, the tin opener for this position is a quite simple move: **1.♖b6xa6+ b7xa6** [1...♔a7-b8 2.♖a6xa8#] leads to an elementary mating position after **2.♕a5-c7#**.
4	After the queen sacrifice **1.♕e2xh5+ ♔h6xh5** the king is in a mate position – therefore: **2.♖b7-h7#**. In the teamwork of Queen + Rook, either the rook or the queen can sacrifice itself to create a mating position.
5	**1.♖g5-h5+** opens the 6th rank and forces the entrapment of the king between his two h-pawns at the same time. **1...g6xh5** allows **2.♕e5-f6#**. *If Black were to move*, he would have three possibilities to give mate: *1...♕f2-f1+* 2.♖g5-g1 ♕f1xf3+ 3.♖g1-g2 ♕f3xg2#; *1...♕f2xf3+* 2.♔h1-g1 ♖d2-d1+ 3.♕e5-e1 ♖d1xe1#; And the easiest way would be *1...♖d2-d1+* 2.♕e5-e1 ♖d1xe1+ 3.♖g5-g1 ♖d1xg1#.
6	Against the apparently safely castled king the sneaky attack **1.♖d8xf8+ ♔g8xf8 2.♕g5-d8#** wins.
7	A king can already be in jeopardy with one open file. But in the fight against two major pieces, two open files definitely mean the end: **1.♖c3-h3+ ♔h8-g7 2.♕e2-g4#**. Also winning is *1.♕e2-h5+ ♔h8-g7* 2.♕h5-g4+ ♔g7-h7 3.♖c3-h3#. This is a typical manoeuvre, where the queen switches files and mate is given on either the g- or the h-file.

8	A *luft* on h7 cannot protect the king from this attack by Rook + Queen: **1.♖e2-e8+ ♔g8-h7 2.♕f3-f5+ g7-g6 3.♕f5xf7#**.
9	Erase everything from your mind except the ♔g8, the g7 pawn, the ♖d8 and the ♘g5, and you will immediately see which motif we have to aim for here. With **1.♕h4-h8+** the queen diverts the king away from the rook, which is unprotected after **1...♔g8xh8**. And after **2.♖d8xf8#** we have our motif on the board!
10	Black is threatening mate on b2 as well as on a1. Unfortunately for him, it is White's move. With **1.♖h1-h8+**, the latter draws the king within reach of the queen, and wins after **1...♔g8xh8** by **2.♕d1-h1+ ♔h8-g8 3.♕h1-h7#**.
11	With **1.♖a1-a8+** the rook diverts the knight, which was blocking the diagonal for the queen. And with this the rook has done enough, as now the queen can force the win quite easily: **1...♘c6-b8 2.♕b5-e8#**.
12	In the previous exercises, either the queen or the rook delivered the mate, but here both have 'equal rights'. The enclosed and cornered king is finished off with either **1.♖h3xh6+ g7xh6 2.♕d2xh6#** or also **1.♕d2xh6+ g7xh6 2.♖h3xh6#**. But if there were no white knight on e6, only the rook sacrifice would lead to victory.

Mate with Queen *against* Rook

Departing from the systematic manner we have been following up to here, we will now have a look at a special tactical situation – the fight of the queen *against* an enemy rook.

Especially on the edge, and if its king is surrounded by the opponent's pawns or his own, the rook is hopelessly inferior to the nimble queen, and it is easily outplayed.

D1 No chance for the rook

In *D1 left*, White wins easily by **1.♕d7-c8+ ♖b6-b8 2.♕c8-c6+ ♖b8-b7 3.♕c6xb7#** [Or 1.♕d7-d8+ ♖b6-b8 2.♕d8-d5+ ♖b8-b7 3.♕c6xb7#]. By the way, this 'trick' also works against a queen!

In *D1 right* the rook doesn't stand a chance either: **1.♕d6-c6+ ♖b8-b7 2.♕c6-c8+ ♖b7-b8 3.♕c8-a6#**.

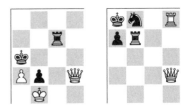

D2 The rook blocks the escape route

Even if the king is not in the corner, he can be threatened with mate, as shown in *D2 left*: **1.♕d5-a8+ ♖c7-a7 2.♕a8-c6#**.

If there are more pieces involved, the number of possibilities grows further. In *D2 right*, **1.♖d8xb8+ ♔a8xb8 2.♕d5-d8#** wins.

Mate with Queen + Bishop

We have already learned a large range of mating possibilities with Queen and Bishop – when we looked at the Mate with Two Bishops!

The queen can always take on the role of the second bishop and, even more than that, with the help of her rook function she can block other escape squares as well. We will not delve deeper into these mating patterns here and only keep in mind that the queen can be more than a substitute for the second bishop.

Our diagrams alongside partly show mating pictures that are also familiar to beginners. Many games end with mate on the square g7 (*D1, D2*).

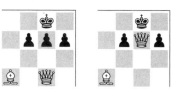

D1 Mate on g7

D2 Mate on g7

The h7-square (*D3*) is another frequent goal of a mating attack by Queen + Bishop.

The 'hole' in the pawn formation in front of the king (*D4*) is created by the fianchetto of the king's bishop, i.e. by moving it to g7. If the bishop is later exchanged off or pursues goals elsewhere on the board, then this hole remains, and it will be a popular target for Queen + Bishop. A hole on g7 not only allows mate on g7, but an additional one on h8 (*D4 left*), which makes the defence more difficult, and sometimes even impossible.

As these attacks – unlike here in the diagram – often come from much further back on the a1-h8 diagonal, they are often hard to recognize.

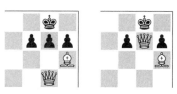

D3 Mate on h7

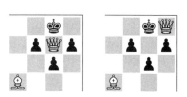

D4 Mate on g7 /on h8 (right)

D5 left shows another version of the mate on g7. Instead of the bishop, a pawn would also do here. *D5 right* shows a weakened castled position, also ending in a mate on g7.

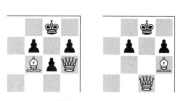

D5 The hole on g7

The queen can not only operate on the diagonal or the vertical lines, as we have seen on the previous page, but also by making use of her rook properties on a horizontal line, i.e., a rank. Anything a rook can do in cooperation with a bishop, the queen also achieves – and more, as *D6* illustrates. A rook would not be of much use here, but the queen wins right away:
1.♕b7xh7#

D6 The Queen on the 7th rank

In *D7*, White makes use of an elementary mating technique. The king is prevented from running away by the white queen. Skilful teamwork by the Bishop + Queen leads to a win by force:
1.♗e4xh7+ [*1.♕h6xh7+?* ♚g8-f8 allows the king to escape] **1...♚g8-h8 2.♗h7-g6+ ♚h8-g8 3.♕h6-h7+** Now everything becomes clear: f7 is the mating square! **3...♚g8-f8 4.♕h7xf7#**

D7 Elementary manoeuvre
leading to mate

Note that this technique only works if f7 is unprotected. But if it is protected, the position is often so constricted that a mate on h8 is possible, as *D8* shows:
1.♕h6xh7+ ♚g8-f8 2.♕h7-h8#
[*1.♗e4xh7+* also works, but it is much more complicated: 1...♚g8-h8 2.♗h7-g6+ ♚h8-g8 3.♕h6-h7+ ♚g8-f8 4.♕h7-h8#]

D8 Mate in the corner

In *D9* we see another standard manoeuvre. White does not give check on h7, but wins at once by:
1.♗f5-e6+ ♚g8-f8 2.♕h5-f7#

D9 Mate on f7

A trick that can only be performed by the queen is shown in *D10*. Here the bishop pins the g7 pawn, which means that for practical purposes the h6-square is unprotected (a pinned piece cannot protect!). The queen does not need an official invitation and rushes to the mating attack:
1.♕f4-h6+ ♚h8-g8 2.♕h6xg7#

D10 Mate exploiting a pin

Quiz 12: Mate with Queen + Bishop

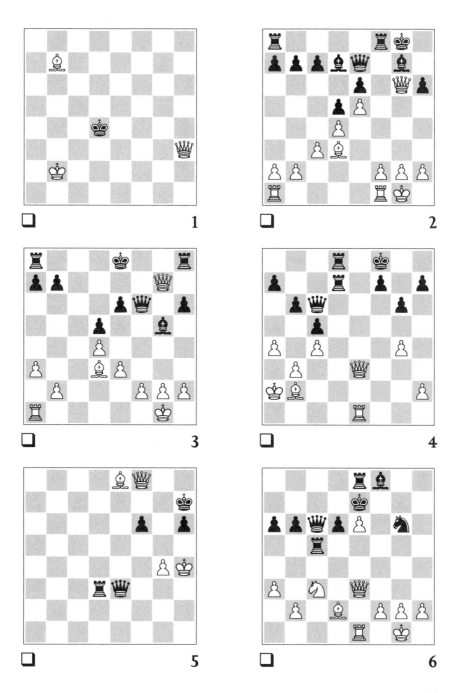

☐   1   ☐   2

☐   3   ☐   4

☐   5   ☐   6

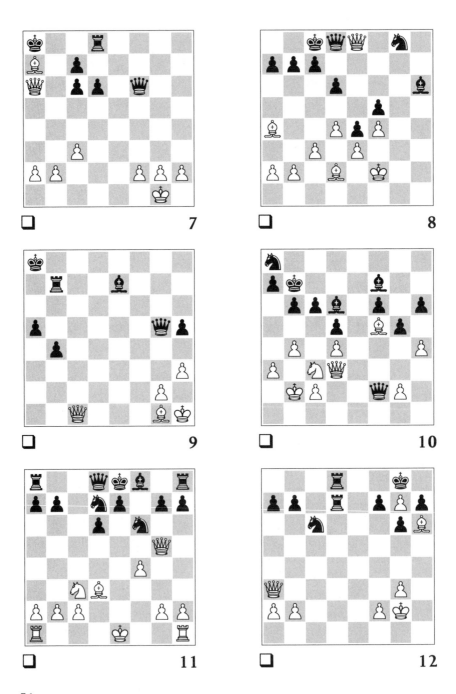

❑ 7

❑ 8

❑ 9

❑ 10

❑ 11

❑ 12

Solutions to 'Mate with Queen + Bishop'

1	Queen + Bishop can always give mate on the edge of the board – and with a little help from their own pieces, or enemy ones that hamper the king, also in the middle of the board: **1.♕h3-c3#**
2	After **1.♕g6-h7+** the king has an escape square, but the bishop rushes up to give mate to him: **1...♔g8-f7 2.♗d3-g6#**
3	Queen + Bishop can quite easily force a king on the edge into a mate position. Here such a situation arises after **1.♗d3-b5+ ♔e8-d8** – the king suddenly finds himself in a mate position: **2.♕g7-d7#**
4	The attack on the long diagonal with **1.♕e3-e5** does not bring White any further here: 1...f7-f6 2.♕e5xf6+ (or also pinning the f6 pawn with 2.♖e1-f1 ♖d7-f7) 2...♕c6xf6 3.♗b2xf6 only nets a pawn and Black will win the endgame. The road to mate leads across a very short diagonal: **1 ♕e3-h6+ ♔f8-g8 2.♕h6-g7#**
5	This time we don't see any combined action by Queen + Bishop – the only function of the latter is to drive the king to the mating square: **1.♗e8-g6+ ♔h7xg6 2.♕f8-g8#** Beginners will probably win from this position in a much more complicated way, e.g.: **1.♕f8-f7+ ♔h7-h8 2.♕f7xf6+ ♔h8-g8 3.♗e8-f7+** Another mating motif – without this move there is no win, only perpetual check! 3...♔g8-f8 (3...♔g8-h7 4.♕f6-g6+ ♔h7-h8 5.♕g6-g8#) 4.♗f7-g6+ ♔f8-g8 5.♕f6-f7+ ♔g8-h8 6.♕f7-h7#/f8# This example shows how you can win games more quickly – or win them at all! – with knowledge of various mating patterns.
6	The queen is the most valuable piece and until now, we have seen her giving mate together with another piece every time. But sometimes you must sacrifice the queen in order to achieve mate with the bishop. That's how it is here: **1.♕e3-g5+ ♖c5xg5** and the bishop overcomes the king, who is surrounded by friend and foe, with **2.♗d2xg5#.**

7	This standard motif you have surely recognized immediately, even though this time it takes place on the queenside: **1.♗a7-b6+ ♚a8-b8 2.♛a6-a7+ ♚b8-c8 3.♛a7xc7#** **1.♗a7-d4+** would have won the queen. You should not immediately rake in the nearest profit, but always look to see if there is an even better move – and giving mate is the best move!
8	Here Black apparently has a solid position and the queen is defending her king. But the pin on the queen enables the bishop to drive away the king: **1.♗a4-d7+ ♚c8-b8 2.♛e8xd8#**
9	It is often already sufficient if the bishop simply cuts off one square and thus limits the mobility of the king: **1.♛c1-c8+ ♖b7-b8 2.♛c8-a6#**
10	This motif is easily overlooked, because it begins with an 'absurd move': **1.♛d3-a6+** Even experienced players often do not consider such moves at first, missing a good mating motif: **1...♚b7xa6** [1...♚b7-c7/b8 2.♛a6-c8#] **2.♗f5-c8#** The queen sacrifice forced the king forward, where he cannot penetrate any further, and the bishop attacked from behind.
11	If you develop as badly in the opening as Black has done here, you may have to reckon with a 'visit' by Queen + Bishop: **1.♛g5-g6+** [or **1.♗d3-g6+** h7xg6 **2.♛g5xg6#**] **1...h7xg6 2.♗d3xg6#** The diagonal e8-h5 is especially vulnerable to attacks by Queen and/or Bishop, and many opening traps are based on the weakness of positions where there is no longer an f-pawn. Here the mistake was the weak move ♘b8-d7 (♘b8-c6 would have been correct), which unnecessarily constricted the king.
12	Here we see the bishop in a special role. It works like an X-ray on the f8-square 'through' the g7 pawn. This enables the queen, after **1.♛a3-f8+ ♖d8xf8 2.g7xf8♛#** (promotion to a rook would also be sufficient), to reappear on the board and immediately give mate!

Mate with Queen + Knight

That which applies for Queen + Bishop or Queen + Rook, applies (almost) just as well here: the queen can always replace a rook or a bishop and thanks to her combination of the properties of these two pieces she can even achieve more.

So all the mating positions with Bishop + Knight or Rook + Bishop are, obviously, also possible with the queen instead of the rook or the bishop. Therefore, we will not repeat these already known positions.

The most frequent occurrences of mate with Queen + Knight are shown in our sub-diagrams alongside.

In *D1*, the knight protects the mating square for the queen, who attacks from the h-file or from the diagonal.

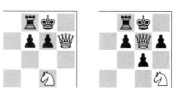

D1 Knight supports the queen

In *D2* as well as *D3*, the knight cuts off the escape square for the king, and the queen gives mate.

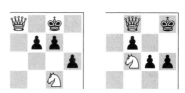

D2 Knight cuts off the escape square

D3 Knight blocks the escape square

In *D4* it is the knight that gives mate, while this time the queen cuts off the escape square(s). Especially the mating position in the sub-diagram on the right is astonishing, and often hard to foresee in practice.

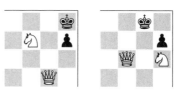

D4 Knight gives mate

A typical manoeuvre can be seen in *D5*. First the queen gives check to drive the king into a mate position, and then with the next check she gives mate:

1.♕b7-f7+ ♚g8-h8 2.♕f7-h7#/f8#

This also works the other way round:

1.♕b7-h7+ ♚g8-f8 2.♕h7-f7#

This manoeuvre is all the more surprising because the king appears to have plenty of free squares around him!

D5 Driving the king into the mate position

Quiz 13: Mate with Queen + Knight

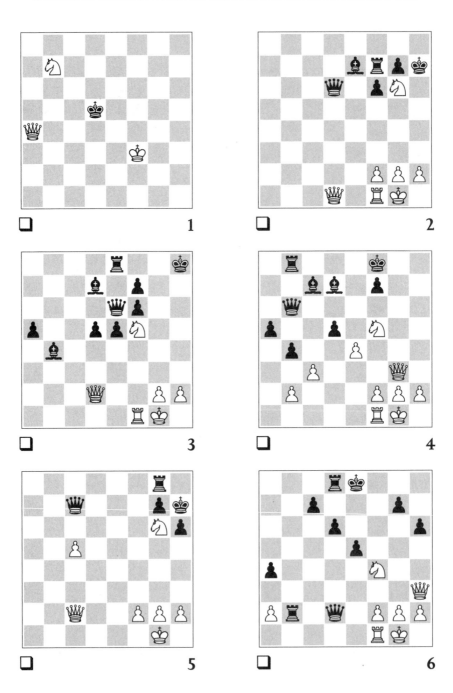

❑ 1

❑ 2

❑ 3

❑ 4

❑ 5

❑ 6

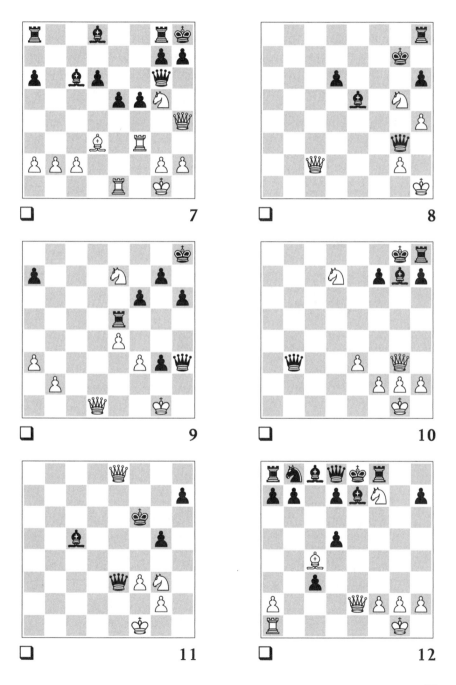

□ 7

□ 8

□ 9

□ 10

□ 11

□ 12

Solutions to
'Mate with Queen + Knight'

1	As with a bishop, in cooperation with a knight the queen can always achieve mate, and if supported by her own pieces or by enemy pieces, she can even do so in the middle of the board. Here the queen is supported by the white king: **1.♕a4-e4#**
2	With the 'bishop move' **1.♕d1-h5+** the queen attacks, and after **1...♔h7-g8** she gives mate with the 'rook move' **2.♕h5-h8#**. A good example of the versatility of the queen, which enables her to exploit the smallest advantages if she is allowed to attack.
3	The open king position invites a queen sortie: **1.♕d2-h6+ ♔h8-g8 2.♕h6-g7#** This time the knight only needed to cover the g7-square for its queen, which is one of its easiest tasks!
4	The knight blocks two important squares: the escape square e7 and g7, on which the queen can enter the position: **1.♕g3-g7+ ♔f8-e8 2.♕g7-g8#**
5	The 'short discovery' **1.♘g6-f8++** utilizes the double check to prepare an inevitable mate: **1...♔h7-h8** and now **2.♕c2-h7#** This is probably the most dangerous discovered attack in the cooperation between Queen + Knight, and it is a nasty surprise in many games!
6	The swiftness of the queen and the manoeuvrability of the knight can lead to spontaneous, utterly surprising mate situations on an open board: **1.♕h3-e6+ ♔e8-f8 2.♘f4-g6#**
7	The mating square h7 is doubly defended and White cannot increase the pressure. On the contrary – his knight is hanging and e5-e4 is threatened, winning a piece. But the boxed-in king in the corner is a perfect target for a mating attack. For this purpose, the queen must be diverted from the protection of the f7-square: **1.♕h4xh7+ ♕g6xh7** and this queen sacrifice is followed by the Smothered Mate **2.♘g5-f7#**.

8	White cannot immediately attack on the kingside, there are too many enemy defenders at the ready there. But a swift switch to the queenside creates new mating possibilities: **1.♕c2-c7+ ♔g7-g6** [or 1...♔g7-f6/f8/g8 2.♕c7-f7#] **2.♕c7-f7#**
9	The knight deprives the king of the escape squares g6 and g8. Now, if you keep an eye on the entire board and call in the queen for reinforcement instead of just bringing the attacked knight into safety, you will win quickly by **1.♕d1-d8+ ♔h8-h7 2.♕d8-g8#**.
10	The pin on the ♗g7 helps you to drive the king into a mate position: **1.♘d7-f6+ ♔g8-f8 2.♕g3-d6#**
11	Queen + Knight do not always manage to give mate. But they can force positions where other pieces can attack successfully: **1.♘g3-h5+ ♔f6-f5** The Queen + Knight tandem cannot make any progress here, e.g. 2.♕e8-f7+ ♔f5-e5 etc., when Black still threatens ...♕f2#. But now that the Queen + Knight have deprived the king of all his squares, the g-pawn can round off the combination: **2.g2-g4#**
12	In confined positions, the queen can pin enemy pieces, and the knight can give mate over the heads of the defenders. Here **1.♘f7-d6#** wins simply. The knight gives check and at the same time cuts off the only free square f7. Instead of the queen, a rook would also suffice.

Decoy, Deflection, Diversion

If, by means of a sacrifice, a piece is forced to go to a certain square, this is called decoy. If it is forced to abandon the protection of a square (see Exercise 7), this is called **deflection**.

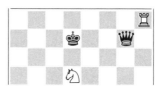

D1 Decoy into a fork

D1 shows a decoy: **1.♖h8-h7 ♕g7xh7** and now the fork **2.♘d5-f6+** is possible.

In *D2* a defender is lured, or deflected, away:
1.♖d5-d8+ ♗e7xd8 2.♖f5-f8#

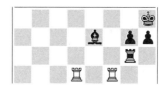

D2 Deflection from the mating square f8

Mate with Bishop + Knight

Without support, Bishop + Knight cannot give mate. *D1 left* shows why this is so. The short-paced knight must be on c6 in order to deprive the king in the corner of the squares a7 and b8. However, in this position it is in the way of the bishop, which could only give the decisive check on b7 – and for that it needs protection, e.g. from its king.

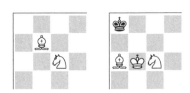

D1 Basic concept

This basic concept is given in *D1 right*. The white king covers the b7-square and thus makes **1.♗a6-b7#** possible.

A king (it could also be a pawn) combined with another piece that blocks an escape square can cause surprising mating positions, as *D2* shows.

D2 Mate on the edge

D3 shows some typical mating positions with kingside castling. The hole on g7 (g2) is a necessary condition here. In both types of position, the bishop can also be standing at a great distance on the diagonal, which makes the mate harder to recognize.

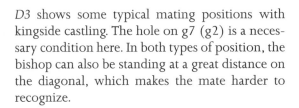

D3 Typical mating positions

Very often the Bishop + Knight achieve their mate with support, direct or indirect, by other pieces. In *D4* it is the queen who sets up the position for the mate by sacrificing herself:

1.♕g6-h7+ ♘f6xh7 2.♘f8-g6#

Without the ♘f6, the queen could immediately give mate on h7.

D4 Queen sacrifice as preparation

D5 shows a mating pattern in positions with a queenside castled king, who is by no means immune against such threats.

We will leave it at these examples.

More than other mating positions, the Mate with Bishop + Knight depends on outside circumstances (= the constellation of your own pieces and your opponent's).

D5 Mate on the queenside

Quiz 14: Mate with Bishop + Knight

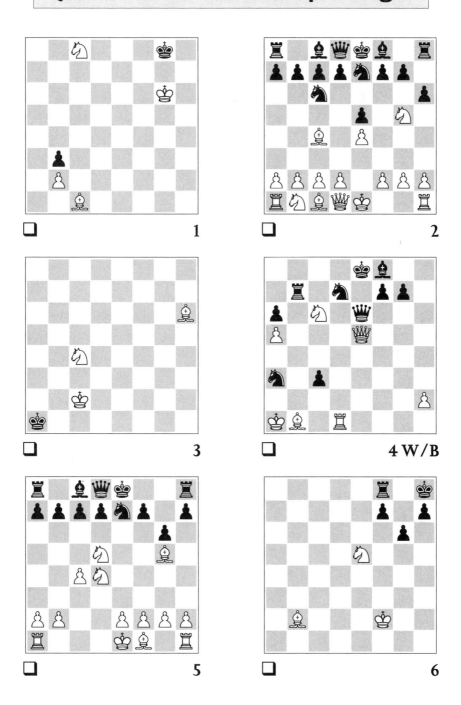

❑ 1

❑ 2

❑ 3

❑ 4 W/B

❑ 5

❑ 6

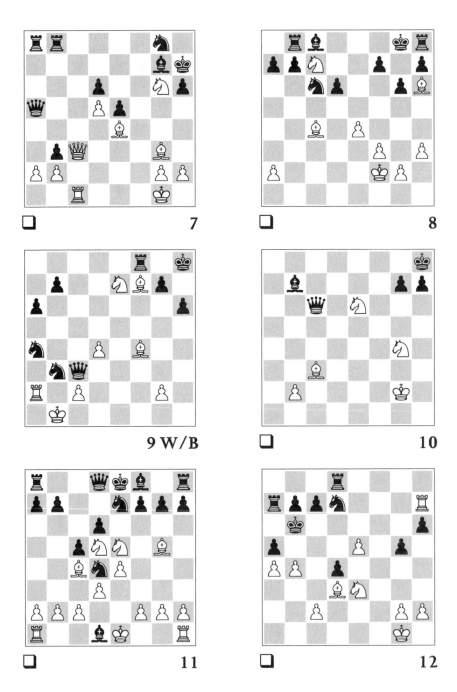

❑ 7

❑ 8

9 W/B

❑ 10

❑ 11

❑ 12

Solutions to 'Mate with Bishop + Knight'

1	Mate is possible not only in the corner, but also on the edge of the board: **1.♗c1-h6 ♔g8-h8 2.♗h6-g7+** (2.♘c8-e7?? stalemate!) **2...♔h8-g8 3.♘c8-e7#**
2	In the opening, if Black plays weakly, the f7-point is a typical target for Bishop + Knight. Here, Black has unnecessarily cramped his position with the weak move ♘g8-e7 (correct would have been ♘g8-f6), and the counterattack on the ♘g5 with h7-h6 comes too late. The game is immediately concluded by **1.♗c4xf7#**
3	There is an important prerequisite for the elementary mate with Bishop + Knight: you can only give mate in the corner where the corner square is of your bishop's colour − the light-squared bishop, in our examples. You must drive the enemy king to this corner, otherwise mate is not possible. In all elementary positions with Bishop + Knight you should play very carefully. If you don't, the king will again get away. Or, even worse, you will stalemate him! This position has one quick solution and a great many slower solutions, of which we will show you one: **1.♔c2-b3 ♔a1-b1 2.♘c4-a3+ ♔b1-a1 3.♗h6-g7#** More complicated is *1.♗h6-f8 ♔a1-a2 2.♘c4-d2 ♔a2-a1 3.♘d2-b3+ ♔a1-a2 4.♘b3-c1+ ♔a2-a1 5.♗f8-g7#*.
4	Many moves have been made since the opening phase, but the black king is still in the middle. Thus, he will fall victim to an attack you'd rather expect to see in the opening: **1.♕e5xe6+ f7xe6 2.♗b1-g6#** *If Black were to move*, he could win: *1...♖b7xb1+ 2.♖d1xb1 ♘a3-c2#*
5	The 'holes' on the kingside (i.e., squares that are not protected by Black and which White can use for his attack) allow one of the typical mating patterns: **1.♘d5-f6+ ♔e8-f8 2.♗g5-h6#**
6	This position shows how strong a bishop on the long diagonal can be − especially if Black is plagued by a fianchetto-hole on g7! **1.♘e5xg6++** Double check! And this is important, because even though *1.♘e5-c6* or *1.♘e5-g4* also created a mate threat, Black would then be able to close the diagonal with 1...f7-f6 and thus ward off all the danger. And after *1.♘e5xf7++?* ♔h8-g8, the white knight would be pinned! **1...♔h8-g8 2.♘g6-e7#**

7	With the double check *1.♘g6-f8++* ♔h7-h8 2.♘f8-g6+ ♔h8-h7 3.♘g6-f8++ etc., White could force a draw by perpetual check. But a slightly different knight manoeuvre leads immediately to mate: **1.♘g6xe5+ ♔h7-h8 2.♘e5-f7#**
8	The black king is already exactly in the right position, and the white knight is brought to bear without delay: **1.♘c7-e8** Black any **2.♘e8-f6#** Or **1.♘c7-d5** and now 1...f7-f5 does not create a real *luft*, since the double check 2.♘d5-f6#/e7# follows.
9	This time mate is not possible, but the position is interesting and the drawing **'move repetition'** (this is the term we use when a piece that moves to and fro forces a draw) should not be kept from the reader. With **1.♘e7-g6+ ♔h8-h7 2.♘g6xf8+ ♔h7-h8 3.♘f8-g6+** White can secure the draw by perpetual check. Of course he could play on, but after, for example, 3.♖a2xa4 or 3.c2xb3 ♕c3-e1+ 4.♗f4-c1 (4.♔b1-c2? ♕e1-e4+) 4...♘a4-c3+, the position is complicated and unclear. *If Black were to move*, he could win quite easily: **1...♕c3-e1+ 2.♗f4-c1 ♕e1xc1#** Or, a little more spectacular, **1...♕c3-b2+ 2.♖a2xb2 ♘a4-c3#** – a pretty mate with the knight pair.
10	Two minor pieces can already cause a lot of commotion on the board, but three or four of them are literally capable of anything, and often they need only little support, or no support at all: **1.♗c3xg7+ ♔h8-g8 2.♘g4-h6#** [But not *2.♘g4-f6+?? ♔g8-f7*]
11	The square f7 is again under fire, but the ♘d5 is in the way of the already familiar mate. As the important ♘e5 is under attack, White has to act quickly and he must not give the black king any possibilities to escape. This is achieved with the move **1.♘d5-f6+**, which brings the desired mating position on the board. After the forced **1...g7xf6**, there follows **2.♗c4xf7#**.
12	In the hustle and bustle of minor pieces, they often get a chance to give mate without warning. Here Black has just moved his pawn away from the attack by the ♘e3 with d5-d4 – and thereby he has brought his own sad end upon himself: **1.♘e3-c4+ ♔b6-c6 2.♗d3-e4#** On (1.♘e3-c4+) **1...♔b6-a6**, this time White does not give a discovered check, but ties up the sack with the simple pawn move 2.b4-b5#. However, if you really want to win with a discovered check, you should (after 1...♔b6-a6) play 2.♖h7xh6+, and you will achieve your aim after 2...b7-b6 [2...c7-c6 3.b4-b5#] with 3.♘c4xa5#.

Part III – More Exercises, Practical Advice and Other Possibilities

By now you have learned a lot about the possibilities to achieve mate with the various pieces, and so we will venture the next step. The practice of the game is much more complicated than our – partly easy – exercises, and now you must learn to recognize mating patterns and apply them in complicated positions. In the beginning you will not be used to doing this, and it is not so easy, but with a little practice you will succeed.

In the chapters 'Mate with Miscellaneous Pieces' and 'Take a Look from the Other Side' you should first have a look at the position. You imagine what could be the threat, look if you can already recognize mating positions, and when you have familiarized yourself with the position (and perhaps even have found a solution already), you should read the comments alongside the position with the solution. Please, read everything, and look at all the variations – not only the moves of the solution!

In the chapter 'How To Crack (Too) Difficult Exercises' you will learn how to divide multiple-move exercises into several shorter ones, and to solve them step by step. Even the longest mating sequence ends with a one-move mate, and we can use this knowledge for our training.

In the rest of the chapters you will receive a number of tips for practical play. Chess consists not only of a knowledge of opening moves and tactical motifs. Just as important are stamina and concentration, patience, the ability to guess your opponent's plans and ideas, and much more. What is the use of spotting a clever combination that wins material, if you play carelessly and inattentively later on and lose everything or miss a mate?

That is why it is important to think before every move, to check all your opponent's moves carefully, and to try and guess their sense and purpose. That is what really makes the game of chess interesting and has been its appeal for hundreds of years!

Mate with Miscellaneous Pieces

In *D1* we see a 'tripling', i.e. White has lined up all three of his major pieces on one file. This is the heaviest artillery that can be brought to bear in a chess game. With so much power, a raid on the back rank is possible, even though it is protected by Black's rook:

1.♖d4-d8+ ♔e8-e7 [1...♖a8xd8 2.♕d3xd8#]
2.♕d3-d7+ ♗c6xd7 3.♖d1xd7#

Often the place which the queen occupies in the tripled line is decisive. If she had been in the foremost position here, a successful attack would not have been possible.

D1 Tripling

In *D2* White has neither doubled nor tripled, and the g8-square is well defended. But another plan is possible, based on the cramped position of the black king:

1.♕g3-g7+ forces **1...♖g8xg7 2.f6xg7+ ♔h8-g8** and the king, who is stuck as if in a vice, has no defence against **3.♘e4-f6#**.

Capturing something is not always the only possibility to achieve a mating attack. There are other ways to win, like decoying the king to a certain square, surrounding him, vacating a square for a new piece, and much more.

D2 Luring forward and clamping

If you can deflect a defender from the back rank just for one move, this will often already decide the game.

In *D3*, the sacrifice **1.♕f5xf7+** deflects the defender for a moment, and after **1...♖f8xf7 2.♖d1-d8+ ♖f7-f8**, the f8-square is attacked twice by the opening of the f-file:
3.♖f1/♖d8xf8#

D3 Temporary deflection

We see two possible mating positions in *D4*: mate with ♖e7 or mate with ♘d4. In both cases the ♘f5 prevents the mate. Capturing it is not the right solution:

1.g4xf5+ g6xf5+ A nasty surprise, and things will get worse: 2.♔g1-f1 ♗c8-a6+ 3.♔f1-e1 (3.♖a7xa6 ♕c6xa6+) 3...♕c6-c1#.

Neither does **1.♖a7-e7+** achieve much for White: 1...♘f5xe7 2.♘f3-d4+ ♔e6-d7 3.♘d4xc6 ♔d7xc6 and Black wins.

1.♘f3-d4+ is the right way. The knight is deflected, and **1...♘f5xd4** is met by **2.♖a7-e7#**.

In such complicated positions, you must play in your head all the moves you can think of (captures, possible checks). Soon you will see what doesn't work, and the road to the win will automatically become apparent – or we find variations that we can calculate further.

D4 Don't get confused!

In *D5* the f8-square is protected, and the king has a *luft*, but after

1.♕f7-f8+ ♗e7xf8 2.♖f1xf8+ ♔h8-h7

all this is of no use because of the double check **3.♘e4-f6#**.

D5 Surprise!

Often it is only a single piece which stands in the way of victory. Here, in *D6*, the g7 pawn protects the f6-square and also blocks the 7th rank for the white rook. Which is a typical overloading situation, as the pawn can only fulfil one of these tasks at a time!

1.♕g5-f6+ (diversion of the g7 pawn) **1...g7xf6**, opening the 7th rank, and now you see the typical mating position after **2.♖h7-f7#**.

D6 Open the 7th rank!

The first mate threat is not always winning. Often it is the prelude to other threats that do achieve the aim.

In D7, **1.♘g7-e8** creates three such threats at the same time: 2.♕f7/♗h6-g7# and 2.♕f7xf8#. The reply **1...♗g5xh6**, which controls both mating squares, seems to fend off all three mate threats, but if we look more closely, we see that in the case of f8 this is only superficially true:
2.♕f7xf8+ ♗h6xf8 and as the knight controls the escape square g7, **3.♖f1xf8#** wins. Black alternatives to 2...♗h6xf8 can only ward off one threat, if at all, and lose quickly.

D7 Queen or Knight?

It can pay off if you study a critical position a bit longer and more closely, as not every mating chance is visible at first sight!

In D8, the rook cuts off the 7th rank for the black king, who is also boxed in by his own pieces. Something should be possible here!

After **1.♕e5-e7+ ♘g8xe7 2.d6xe7+** the king only has two squares, both of which, however, can be attacked by the knight: **2...♔f8-e8/g8 3.♘e4xf6#**

D8 King in a fix

In *D9*, inexperienced players would probably play *1.♘h4-f5* ♖e8-g8 2.e6-e7 ♕b6-b4 (preventing ♖e1), and the fight would go on, with an unclear outcome (on 2...♖a8-e8? 3.♘f5-d6 wins the exchange, with an advantage).

But there is a simple recipe for victory: open the h-file and mate the boxed-in king:
1.♘h4-g6+ h7xg6 2.♖f1-f3 (such 'quiet moves' are easily overlooked) Black any, and now **3.♖f3-h3#**

D9 Open the h-file!

A protected piece is not necessarily safe. In *D10*, the ♖e5 is protected, but if we look closer we can establish that despite the difference in value of 5:9 points, White can nevertheless advantageously capture it with the queen.

The reason is that after **1.♕c3xe5+ ♖e8xe5**, the brief deflection from the back rank will cost Black dearly: **2.♖b1-b8+ ♖e5-e8 3.♖b8xe8#**

D10 Protected, but not taboo!

In *D11* the solid wall of black defenders seems to be impenetrable. But a cheeky manoeuvre, based on two mating motifs, secures the win:

1.♕g5-h6 Threatening **♕xg7#** – the first mating motif [1...g7xh6 2.♘f5xh6# – the second mating motif]. **1...♕e6-f6** The only possibility to fend off the mate threat, but not for long:

2.♗b2xf6 ♘e4/g7xf6 3.♕h6-/xg7#

[2...g7xh6 is again met by 3.♘f5xh6#]

D11 A cheeky manoeuvre

In *D12* the black queen has captured the rook on a1. That's all well and good, but it would have been better if Black had paid more attention to the safety of his king.

After **1.♕e7xf8+ ♔g8xf8 2.♗e3-c5+**, the discovering bishop not only opens up the rook file, it also drives the king back into his hole: **2...♔f8-g8**, and this allows the back-rank mate **3.♖e1-e8#**.

D12 Optimistic rook capture

Look at the Entire Board!

Many inexperienced players will only look at the left side of the board in *D1*. They move their king forward in order to force the promotion. This may work, or it may not – this type of endgame is hard to calculate even for experienced players. However, all these deliberations are not necessary here, because if we look at the entire board, we will see that the black king is in a mate position, and so White can simply play **1.♖a1-b1**, since **1...♖a8xa7?** fails immediately to **2.♖b1-b8#**. And 1...f7-f5 is too slow, for then the direct 2.♖b1-b8+ follows, and White wins.

D1 A simple and clear win?

The situation in *D2* appears to be more complicated. With **1.♕e4xe5** White wins a pawn, brings the bishop into play and either forces an endgame or threatens to start a mating attack (e.g. with ♕e8+): 1...♕b2xe5 2.♘g6xe5 ♖f7-e7 3.♗f3-d5+ ♔g8-g7 4.♘e5-c6, with a worse endgame. In these considerations, everything revolves around the win of the pawn and the later pawn hunt on the queenside, in order to improve the material balance or increase the drawing chances. (For the endgame there is a rule: If all pieces are on one wing, the chances increase for the weaker side. The king can defend himself more effectively, and many pawn endgames can be held to a draw.)

D2 The solution is far away

If you look at the entire board, you will see that there are possibilities on the back rank. First the queen must leave the battle scene: **1.♕e4-a8+ ♔g8-g7** [1...♖f7-f8 2.♕a8xf8#] and now – no pawn gain, no endgame, but there is **2.♕a8-h8#**. Very, very often, the solution to a problem can be found not in the immediate vicinity of the battle scene, but far away; for example, a piece can be brought closer – or it involves a distant square, as in our examples, or it may simply mean that you should play on the other wing if you cannot make any progress with an attack on the king. So – always look at the entire board, not only part of it!

94

Every Move Has Sense!

Except when playing against outright beginners, every chess player should assume that his opponent's moves are based on a logical sense and purpose. Chess is a battle of plans. With every move a small plan is drawn up, and hopes and expectations are connected. This already starts on the second move, when after **1.e2-e4 e7-e5** White attacks the king's pawn with **2.♘g1-f3**.

Most plans made during a game lead nowhere, because the opponent thwarts them – consciously or unconsciously. In our example, he plays **2...♘b8-c6**, after which the white knight can no longer win the pawn.

A new plan is introduced with **3.d2-d4** *(D1)* – either to win the e5 pawn, which is now attacked twice and protected only once, or to push the d-pawn and attack/drive away the ♘c6 in order to remove it from the centre, at the same time creating space for White's own pieces, etc.

D1 after 3.d2-d4

The first plan consisted of only one threat (♘f3xe5), but the next plan already contains numerous options – apart from those mentioned above, another idea is to bring other pieces (the bishop, the queen) into the game. A chess game is a continuous chain of plans and counteractions by both players, until one of them doesn't pay attention or does not know a certain theme (e.g., a threatened mate), allowing his opponent to successfully carry through a plan. If both players know a lot about chess and remain alert, it is probable that the game will end in a draw.

In *D2*, the knight attacks the a-pawn. White reacts with **1.c2-c3**. This should rouse the black player's suspicion. Why does White give up one of his pawns? Why doesn't he simply play *1.a2-a3*, also attacking the knight and saving his pawn as well?

If you fail to find the answer, you will learn something new after **1...♘b4xa2?? 2.♔d2-c2** followed by ♔b1, – but you will lose a piece, and probably the game.

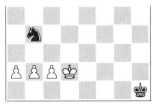

D2 White plays c2-c3

Two basic rules should be observed:

- **With every move you should strive for something, prepare, plan something, with the aim of obtaining an advantage.**

If no clear plan presents itself, you should try to improve your position a little. Perhaps the placement of a certain piece can be improved? If a minor piece is still on your first rank, it may be possible to develop it and thereby connect the rooks on the first rank, which will protect you against many mate threats. Making a luft for the king is hardly ever wrong. However, take care when you push pawns, for as you know they cannot move backwards and pushing them forward may weaken your position!

- **With every move by your opponent, you should also investigate his possibilities, his intentions, changes in the position, etc.**

The best plan for you will be of no use if your opponent can carry through his plan faster. If, for instance, both players are planning a promising mating attack, he whose plan works first (i.e. he who gives mate), wins. From this we can learn the following:

- **Recognizing your opponent's plans is more important than making your own.**

Beginners often lose very quickly against experienced players, because they do not recognize their plans – or they don't until it's too late to save themselves!

- **'Gifts' by the opponent, tempting wins of pieces or pawns, should always arouse our suspicion. Perhaps it is an oversight by the opponent, but it may also be a trap.**

Experienced players make relatively few 'big mistakes', so with them the probability of a trap is much higher than is the case with weak opponents.

Especially if your opponent does not react to an obvious threat, you should think sharply what he may be up to. Merrily carrying on with your own plan is often the surest road to a loss!

So, before every move you make, think carefully what your opponent's plans may be, and if they could become dangerous for you!

Only if this is clear should you start pursuing your own plans!

Zugzwang

In chess White and Black alternate their moves. This is fair, and mostly it is a good thing, but not always. Sometimes a player has a position where he couldn't be beaten if it were **not** his move, whereas any move he makes will mean disaster for him.

This is demonstrated by a typical example from a King + Rook versus King ending. In *D1*, Black is to move on both sides. In the diagram positions themselves White could not harm him, but on the only possible move **1...♔b1-a1** (1...♔h2-h1), there follows **2.♖c3-c1#** (2.♖f3-h3#). Zugzwang has decided the game.

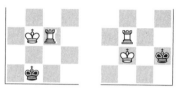

D1 Black is in zugzwang

In *D2* zugzwang also decides the issue. After **1.♔e6-f7** nothing could happen to Black if only it were not his move, since White cannot increase the pressure. The only black piece that can move protects the mate square g7 – and it has to move away! **1...♗h6-e3** is an ultimate attempt to divert the opponent and at least save the draw, but: **2.♗d4xg7#**.

D2 White creates zugzwang

Also in *D3* White can achieve zugzwang by making the right move.
1.♘d5-b6? deprives the black king of his last square, but blocks the b-pawn and thus gives stalemate! **1.♔c8-c7** would introduce a long-winded manoeuvre, which wins in the end.
1.♘d5-c7 is the right way.
Black is in zugzwang. His two only (practically equivalent) moves lose immediately. If he didn't have to move, White could not win immediately. But here, on **1...b7-b5** [or 1...b7-b6], **2.c5/a5xb6#** decides.
This should be enough for now. Further on, in endgame training, you will learn much more about zugzwang, a factor which is one of the most important cornerstones of the endgame, and which keeps appearing time and time again in that phase.

D3 White to move

How to Crack (Too) Difficult Exercises The '3-Circle Training'

Combinations can go on for many moves, sometimes even more than ten! How can you calculate all this in your head?

'I will never learn this!', many a chess friend will sigh. But you can! The trick is that even the longest mating combination ends with a mate in 1, 2, 3 moves. If we detect such a short, simple combination as a possibility on the board, we already have the key to the solution in our hands. And we can practise this during training sessions. We can divide a long combination into several shorter ones, and this way we can solve the exercise step by step. First an example:

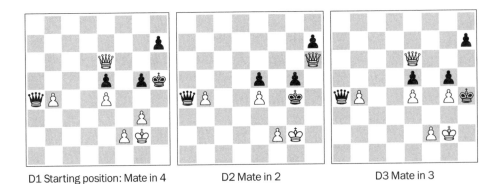

D1 Starting position: Mate in 4   D2 Mate in 2   D3 Mate in 3

The starting position *D1* is not so easy to fathom for an inexperienced player. Probably he will continue giving checks with the queen, until either a mate will occur by coincidence or the game is agreed drawn.

If we divide the exercise into parts, even a beginner will already have much less trouble finding the solution (*D2*): **1.♕h6-h3+ ♚g4-f4 2.♕h3-f3/f5#**

After the next step, a solution in 3 moves (*D3*), the winning plan should be detectable: **1.♕e6-h6+ ♚h4xg4 2.♕h6-h3+ ♚g4-f4 3.♕h3-f3/f5#**

In *D1* White must drive the king in the direction of his own king position. There he will be mated quickly, locked in by his own pawns and the opponent's. Thus: **1.g3-g4+ ♚h5-h4 2.♕e6-h6+ ♚h4xg4 3.♕h6-h3+ ♚g4-f4 4.♕h3-f3/f5#**

The pawn sacrifice to drive the king to g4 was the decisive idea, but in order to venture such a move you must recognize the simple mating patterns. For this purpose, Frank Oltman has developed a training programme, the '**3-Circle Training**' (see under 'Additional Material and Tools' at the end of this book).

This is an excellent aid to make the jump from shorter to longer combinations easier, and to learn certain playing techniques at the same time. If you see a tactical exercise that you cannot solve, ask someone to divide it into one or two shorter combinations for you. Then you try to solve the shortest of them. This will show you the elementary mating motif, which is the basis of the entire combination. Normally speaking, the middle exercise and the final solution should not be a problem. Below we give a few more examples for the '3-Circle Training': first we give the 2-move mates, then the sub-exercises with 3 moves, and finally the original 4-move exercises. The order of the exercises is mixed, so as not to make it too easy for you.

1st Step – Mate in 2 moves

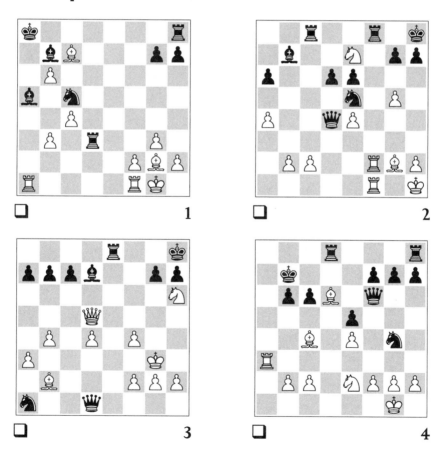

1

2

3

4

2nd Step – Mate in 3 moves

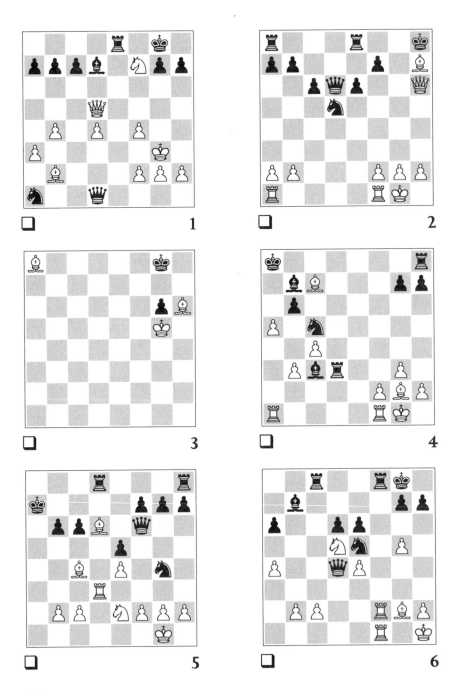

1

2

3

4

5

6

3rd Step – Mate in 4 moves

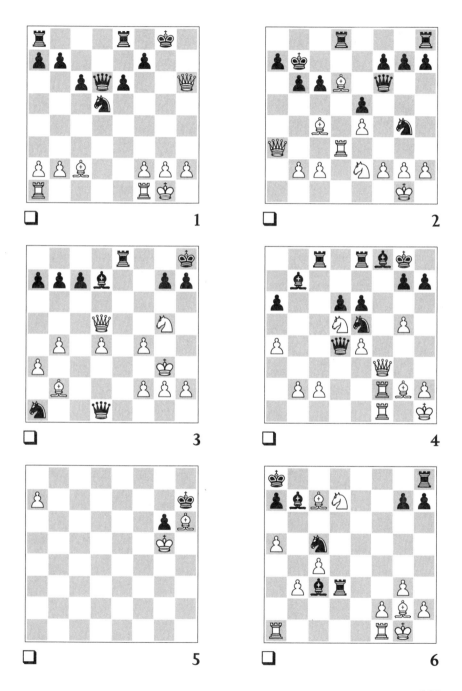

❑ 1

❑ 2

❑ 3

❑ 4

❑ 5

❑ 6

Solutions to 'The 3-Circle Training'

First Step – Mate in 2 moves

1	The first question should always be: can I capture a piece, or is there a trick in the position? Don't worry, there is no trick here, so here we go: **1.♖a1xa5+ ♘c5-a6 2.♖a5xa6#**
2	This simple back-rank mate you had surely spotted right away: **1.♖f2xf8+ ♖c8xf8 2.♖f1xf8#**
3	You surely remember this position that is typical for the Smothered Mate: **1.♕d5-g8+ ♖e8xg8 2.♘h6-f7#**
4	As so often, the solution here is a mix of motifs. Here the motifs of 'Mate with Two Bishops' and 'Rook + Bishop – discovery with control of an escape square' apply: **1.♗c4-a6+ ♔b7-a8 2.♗a6-c8#**

Second Step – Mate in 3 moves

1	With the discovered check White cannot win material, but it does suffice for mate: **1.♘f7-h6+** [*1.♘f7-d6+?* ♗d7-e6] **1...♔g8-h8** [1...♔g8-f8?? 2.♕d5-f7#] **2.♕d5-g8+ ♖e8xg8 3.♘h6-f7#**
2	The mate with Queen + Discovering Bishop is an elementary mating technique: **1.♗h7-g6+ ♔h8-g8 2.♕h6-h7+ ♔g8-f8 3.♕h7xf7#**
3	If the enemy king is so constricted and his only pawn is blocked, you should always be wary of potential stalemates. Therefore, always check if after the move you are planning the enemy king can still make a move! **1.♔g5xg6** [*1.♗a8-d5+* also wins, but this line is more complicated: 1...♔g8-h8 2.♔g5-f6 (2.♔g5xg6?? stalemate) 2...♔h8-h7 3.♗h6-g7 g6-g5 4.♔f6-f7 g5-g4 5.♗d5-e4#] **1...♔g8-h8 2.♗h6-g7+ ♔h8-g8 3.♗a8-d5#**

4	**1.a5xb6+** The opening of the file finishes off the boxed-in king: **1...♗c3-a5** [Or 1...♗c3xa1 2.♖f1xa1+] **2.♖a1xa5+ ♘c5-a6 3.♖a5xa6#**
5	The rook takes possession of the open a-file and supports the bishop pair: **1.♖d3-a3+ ♔a7-b7 2.♗c4-a6+ ♔b7-a8 3.♗a6-c8#**
6	The ♖f8 is attacked by two pieces, and defended by two of its own pieces. This equilibrium is broken by **1.♘d5-e7+**, forcing one of the defenders to move away. The end is swift: **1...♔g8-h8 2.♖f2xf8+ ♖c8xf8 3.♖f1xf8#** [By the way, first **1.♖f2xf8+ ♖c8xf8** and then **2.♘d5-e7+ ♔g8-h8** would have lead to the same result.]

Third Step – Mate in 4 moves

1	As the bishop comes to the aid of the queen, a quick and certain win is possible: **1.♗c2-h7+ ♔g8-h8 2.♗h7-g6+ ♔h8-g8 3.♕h6-h7+ ♔g8-f8 4.♕h7xf7#**
2	The many white pieces do not help, as long as the king can hide behind his a7 pawn. So, that one has to go first: **1.♕a3xa7+** [*1.♕a3-a6+* leads to the same position as in the main line after 1...♔b7-a8 2.♕a6xa7+ ♔a8xa7] **1...♔b7xa7** Now the rest is easy: occupy the open file, bring the second bishop into play and then the mate will follow almost automatically: **2.♖d3-a3+ ♔a7-b7 3.♗c4-a6+ ♔b7-a7/a8 4.♗a6-c8#**
3	The Smothered Mate with its typical starting position is easy to recognize, and you will surely find the solution like a shot: **1.♘g5-f7+ ♔h8-g8 2.♘f7-h6+ ♔g8-h8 3.♕d5-g8+ ♖e8xg8 4.♘h6-f7#**
4	The ♗f8 is attacked three times, and it is also defended three times. But at the decisive moment, White can break this equilibrium and achieve victory: **1.♕f3xf8+ ♖e8xf8 2.♖f2xf8+** [*2.♘d5-e7+* is a transposition we have seen with the second step] **2...♖c8xf8 3.♘d5-e7+ ♔g8-h8 4.♖f1xf8#**

5	Here you cannot simply triumphantly put a queen on the board (nor a rook), as then Black will be the one to rejoice – in stalemate! Only a minor piece comes into consideration – and since giving mate is much easier and faster with the bishop pair than with Bishop + Knight, the choice is not too difficult, especially since the king is already in the corner as well: **1.a7-a8♗** Underpromotion! **1...♔h7-g8** [or also 1...♔h7-h8 2.♔g5xg6 ♔h8-g8 3.♗a8-d5+ ♔g8-h8 4.♗h6-g7#] **2.♔g5xg6 ♔g8-h8 3.♗h6-g7+ ♔h8-g8 4.♗a8-d5#**
6	In order to get to the king in the corner, White has to open either the long diagonal or the a-file, and take control of it. **1.♘d7xc5 ♗b7xg2 2.♘c5xd3 ♗g2xf1 3.♖a1xf1** would give White some advantage, but it would not achieve any of these aims. Therefore: **1.♘d7-b6+ a7xb6 2.a5xb6+** and now Black can only postpone the inevitable: **2...♗c3-a5** [Or 2...♗c3xa1 3.♖f1xa1+] **3.♖a1xa5+ ♘c5-a6 4.♖a5xa6#** Well, that wasn't so hard, was it? You should be able to solve the 4-movers easily after having seen the mating motif in the shorter exercises. Have no fear of long solutions, they always end in a simple mate that you already know!

Take a Look from the Other Side

Up to here we have seen only positions where White was to move. However, this certainly does not mean that White is the only one who can win by tactics. Black's chances are just as good. Most of the mating patterns function equally well with both colours. Of course, thanks to his first move, White will be able to attack a little earlier in the opening, and therefore some mating patterns are more frequently, or even almost exclusively, produced by White. The Scholar's Mate, which occurs after the moves **1.e2-e4 e7-e5 2.♕d1-h5 ♘b8-c6 3.♗f1-c4 ♘g8-f6 4.♕h5xf7#**, is a simple example. When does Black ever achieve a Scholar's Mate?

The simple reason for our preference for White was that, when setting up the positions on the chessboard, you wouldn't have to turn the board around every time. Moreover, it is easier when you concentrate on one colour and look at all the positions from White's point of view.

But now you are not a beginner any more, and when we present a series of black positions, you won't have to rotate the board.

If you set up the positions on the chessboard, you can look at them from either Black's or White's point of view, that is merely a question of taste. However, in diagrams in chess books, the positions are almost without exception shown from White's point of view, and if you have already made so much progress that you can solve most positions from a sheet, you should get accustomed to that right away.

At this opportunity, we want to have a look at a few motifs that have not, or only briefly, been dealt with so far.

First have a good look at the diagram of each exercise and think what could be possible, what threats there are, etc. Only when you have established a certain impression of the position for yourself – possibly you have even acquired an idea of the solution – you should look at the solution. Do not look at the solution move only, but play through all the sidelines and alternative solutions as well. This way you will learn many extra things without effort!

In *D1* White has protected the squares d1 and g2, on which mate could be threatened. But he has overlooked **1...♛d5-h1#**.

That's bad luck, since with **1.♖f5xg5+** h6xg5 (or 1...♚g8-h8 2.♕h3xh6#) **2.♕h3-h7#** White could even have won.

D1

Please note: Even if you have a great attacking plan, you should always check what your opponent is up to!

If you want to establish whether an attack will be successful, you usually count the number of attackers and defenders, and if this number is equal, the attack will not push through. You should also take into account which pieces can be interposed.

In *D2*, the c1-square is twice attacked and twice defended. So, will the attack fail?

No – you should never forget that a pinned piece (in this case, the knight) cannot be counted! Also, the ♗b2 is pinned, and it cannot move to b1. Therefore we have a green light for:

1...♕c7-c1+ 2.♖h1xc1 ♖c8xc1#

D2

If you think too sophisticatedly, this will prevent you from seeing the mate in *D3* due to all the major pieces standing around. You should imagine what a mate to the white king could look like, and then you will find the solution:

1...♖b3-a3+ (line clearance) **2.♖a4xa3** and now the elementary mate **2...♕b5-b2#**

D3

106

In *D4*, among other things, it is also important to see the entire board, as the pieces that are important for the attack do not stand in the immediate vicinity of the white king, but are at a great distance:

1...♖a8-a1+ decoys the king from the escape square c2, into the corner. **2.♔b1xa1** and now, with the support of the ♗e6, **2...♕b3-a2#** wins.

D4

A king in the corner always lives dangerously – and often not very long – no matter if he is white or black! In *D5* Black has a lot of free space, which is not something that can be said of the white king. And lo and behold, he is done in with a version of the Smothered Mate:

1...♕d6xh2+ 2.♖c2xh2 ♘h5-g3#

D5

With a double check it doesn't matter if the opponent is attacking either one of the checking pieces, or even both – after all, he has no time to capture either of them. This is Black's luck in *D6*, since after **1...♘f3-d4+** both of his pieces are hanging and the only possible reply **2.♔e2-e1** leads directly to mate: **2...♘d4-c2#**

A heavily confined king position is especially dangerous if the opponent can bring several minor pieces to bear against it, or if he has a space advantage (e.g. thanks to a constricting pawn).

D6

107

In *D7* Black's queen and knight are under attack. But that doesn't matter:

1...♕f2-f1+ 2.♖g2-g1 ♘f5-g3+!

Now all that remains is **3.h2xg3**, when the queen makes use of the open h-file by playing **3...♕f1-h3#**.

We had a similar position in the chapter 'Mate with Queen against Rook'.

Transposition is not possible:

1...♘f5-g3+?? 2.♖g2xg3 and White wins easily, as he is threatening 3.♕e4-e8+ ♔h8-h7 4.♕e8-g6+ ♔h7-h8 5.♕g6xg7#.

D7

1...♘d2xb3+ gives a double check, which is often decisive. But in *D8* it brings Black nothing, since after 2.♔c1-b1 he has no good follow-up.

Instead, **1...♘c5xb3+** forces the line clearance **2.c2xb3** and now the double check **2...♘d2xb3#** is decisive thanks to the support from the bishop pair.

If you see a tactical opportunity like a double check, do not jump at it, but always make sure that it is really useful to you! All that glitters is not gold!

D8

The queen sacrifice **1...♕b8xb2+ 2.♖b1xb2** forces the rook into a pin by the ♗f6, and thus makes it impossible for it to defend the back rank. This proves fatal:

2...♖e8-e1+ 3.♕d5-d1 ♖e1xd1#

D9 The queen sacrifice

In *D10* White is threatening three mates at the same time: on a8, b7 and with 2.♖h8+. And his king is really well wrapped up. Perhaps a little too well!?

1...♘f5-g3+ 2.h2xg3 Line clearance is almost without exception the best recipe for the attacker. Apart from the knight, the other pieces can only get to the king when he is 'accessible'!

2...♖f4-h4+ 3.g3xh4 ♕b4xh4+ 4.♖h7xh4 ♖a4xh4#

D10

Inexperienced players often lose concentration when they believe that their position is already as good as winning or losing. In both cases this is wrong, because there are often still surprising chances in the position. What was that old trainer's wisdom again: 'It ain't over till it's over!'

In *D11* Black, who is already (as good as) defeated, manages to land a counterblow:

1...♘h3-f2+ 2.♔h1-h2 ♗g7-e5#

And now it's over!

D11

1...♕f5xf2+ forces the opening of the e-file in *D12* and thus brings the ♖e8 into play.

2.♘e4xf2 [2.♔g1-h1 ♕f2-f1#/e1#]

While the knight controls the escape square h2, the rook can conquer the unprotected back rank, finishing the game with **2...♖e8-e1#**.

D12

An open f-file = weakened diagonal in the direction of the ♔g1, Queen + Knight in the vicinity of the enemy king's position – aren't your fingers already itching to conjure up a Smothered Mate on the board in *D13*?

1...♕d2-e3+ 2.♔g1-h1 ♘d3-f2+ 3.♔h1-g1 [3.♖f1xf2 ♕e3-e1+ 4.♖f2-f1 ♕e1xf1#] 3...♘f2-h3+ 4.♔g1-h1 ♕e3-g1+ 5.♖f1xg1 ♘h3-f2#

D13

The white e5 pawn attacks the queen in *D14*. This should not entice us to automatically move it away. Instead, we must first check what this position has to offer. The white king is cut off from g1 by the ♗c5, and after an opening of the h-file by **1...♘e4xg3+ 2.h2xg3**, this enables Black to play **2...♕f6-h6+ 3.♔g2-h3 ♕h6xh3#**.

Against a king in the corner, opening lines is almost always the right method!

D14

In *D15* the surprising move **1...♖d4-h4+** forces either **2.g3xh4**, when the weakening of the defending pawns in front of the king allows the elementary mate **2...♕d5-f3#**; or **2.♔h3xh4** and now the quite simple **2...♕d5-h5#**.

D15

I hope you have not fallen into despair looking for a mate in *D16*, as this time it cannot be forced.

After **1...♘f6xe4** White cannot take the queen, otherwise **2.♗g5xd8 ♗c5xf2#** will follow. His only remedy is 2.♗g5-e3 ♗c5xe3 3.d3xe4 (or 3.f2xe3 ♘e4-f6) 3...♗e3-c5 and White gets away with the loss of a pawn.

Instead of this mate trap, also possible is **1...♗c5xf2+** 2.♔e1xf2 (or 2.♔e1-d2 ♘f6xe4+ 3.d3xe4 ♕d8xg5+) 2...♘f6-g4+ 3.♔f2-e1 ♕d8xg5.

The difference is that Black does not even try to set the trap, but instead weakens White's position heavily by depriving him of the right to castle.

D16

Many king positions are like a cave. If you can lure the king away from the entrance, he can be trapped.

This is done in *D17* by **1...♕b5-b1+**, which forces the king into a mate position: **2.♔c1xb1 ♖d8-d1#**

And that was the best defence against the threat of ♕h6-g7#.

D17

'**Boden's Mate**', named after an English master who applied it for the first time around 1850, is a deadly mating attack on a queenside-castled king. By motif this is a two-bishop mate, which is introduced by a sacrifice (mostly of a queen or a rook).

1...♕f6xc3+ 2.b2xc3 ♗f8-a3#

D18 Boden's Mate

If Black in *D19* could concentrate his rooks and queen on the open h-file, this would guarantee him the win. But he has no time for this. The recipe for this problem was already found in 1512 by the Portuguese pharmacist Pedro Damiano!

1...♖h8-h1+ 2.♔g1xh1 ♖d8-h8+ 3.♔h1-g1 ♖h8-h1+4.♔g1xh1

One rook after the other is 'relieved from its duties', to allow the queen to finally intervene:

4...♕c8-h8+ 5.♔h1-g1

[White can avoid mate in two by ingeniously interposing the queen with 5.♕e2-h5, but after 5...♕h8xh5+ 6.♔h1-g1 ♕h5-h2+ 7.♔g1-f1 ♕h2-h1+ 8.♔f1-e2 his king is still caught: 8...♕h1xg2+ 9.♔e2-e1 ♕g2-f2+ 10.♔e1-d1 g3-g2 followed by 11...g2-g1♕+ and mate]

5...♕h8-h2+ 6.♔g1-f1 ♕h2-h1#

D19

The plan that was used in *D3* of the 'Double check' chapter (see page 38), can also be applied in this position D20. Often the problem is that you must be able to recognize such positions with reversed colours.

Black wins by **1...♕a4-d1+ 2.♔c1xd1 ♗d7-a4++ 3.♔d1-e1**

[**3.♔d1-c1?** ♖d8-d1# A typical Rook + Bishop mate]

3...♖d8-d1+ 4.♘e3xd1 and a mate with Bishop + Knight concludes the combination:

4...♗h6-d2#

D20

1...♘e4xg3+ 2.f2xg3 Black could now liquidate into a probably winning endgame:

2...♕f5xf1+ 3.♕e1xf1 ♘e2xg3+ 4.♔h1-g1 ♘g3xf1 5.♔g1xf1 ♖h8xh3 etc.

Or **2...♘e2xg3+ 3.♔h1-g1** (3.♕e1xg3?? ♕f5xf1#) **3...♕f5xf1+ 4.♕e1xf1 ♘g3xf1 5.♔g1xf1 ♖h8xh2.**

But an intermediate move, also often called a 'zwischenzug', immediately forces the white king into a mate position:

2...♖h8xh2+! 3.♔h1xh2 ♕f5-h7#

D21

Actually this book only deals with mating attacks, but I couldn't resist showing this example.
1...&c5xf2+ poses problems for White:
2.&e1xf2 &f6-g4+ 3.&f2-e1 [3.&f2-f1 allows the fork 3...&g4-e3+ 4.&f1-e1 &e3xd1]
3...&g4-e3 and the queen (!) is mated!
The best continuation is **2.&e1-f1**, e.g. 2...0-0! and with the loss of the right to castle, a boxed-in rook and bad developing chances, the game has not started out well for White.

D22

In *D23* White has put his faith in the fact that **1...&e8xe2** cannot be played in view of the mating attack **2.&c5-c8+** (not 2.&c1xe2?? &a5-e1#) 2...&e2-e8 3.&c8xe8#.
However, he has overlooked **1...&a5-e1+**. The &e8 X-rays the square e1 through the &e2, and Black achieves mate after **2.&e2xe1 &e8xe1#**.
Inexperienced players should preferably not build their game on complicated plans!

D23

Though the advantage of the first move by nature gives White a little more tactical possibilities than his opponent, it doesn't protect him from falling victim to traps and mating motifs.
In *D24* White has played the weak move &g1-e2. The knight is standing in the way of the queen, king and bishop, and it allows Black's minor pieces a lot of space in the middle of the board. This immediately has fatal consequences:
1...&d4-f3#

D24

Part IV – The Great Test

Bravo! You have (almost) made it through this book, and now you should be a real expert in mating the king! In this concluding great test you can find out how well you have really understood everything, and what you may still be missing or may have forgotten.

But our 60 test exercises are also intended to provide further knowledge, and the points you score are of secondary importance only.

In order to solve 60 exercises, you need a lot of time and good condition. This is not possible for everyone, and it would overtax younger readers especially. Therefore it makes sense to divide the test in e.g. 2 x 30 or 3 x 20 exercises, and solve these in the space of several days.

Adult readers, however, should try to work through the entire test in one go. Then it will also serve as a good training of your condition and your concentration, and as a simulation of the practice of tournament chess.

There is no suggested time limit for the individual exercises, but if you still haven't found a solution after a maximum of 5 minutes, you should move on to the next exercise and perhaps have another look at this one later on. An egg-timer is a helpful device to avoid excessive brooding!

As earlier on, in Part III, all the solutions should be carefully played through and studied – you should not merely look at the solution and jot down your points! For recording the points you will find a solution sheet on page 137, where you can fill in the key move and, at a later stage, your score. However, for writing down the complete solution it is best to use a scratch-pad, where you can record the winning lines in a nice and readable way.

The Evaluation on page 138 provides you with a number of practical suggestions for further training along the way, as does the next chapter 'Additional Material and Tools', where you will be handed directions for further training material.

And now, enough talk – pitch in and have fun with our Great Test!

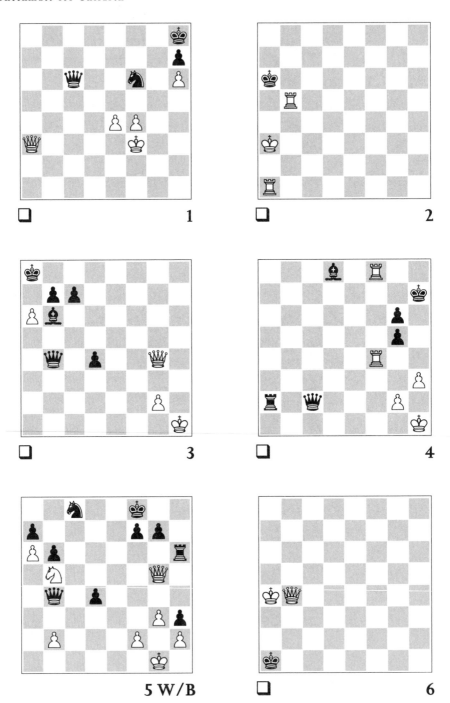

1

2

3

4

5 W/B

6

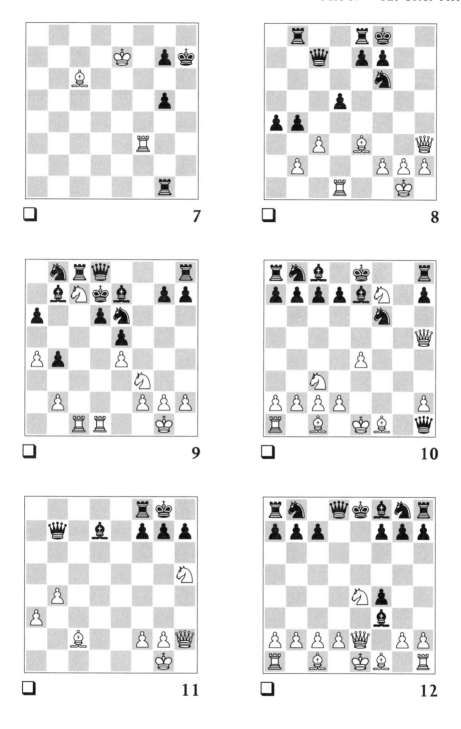

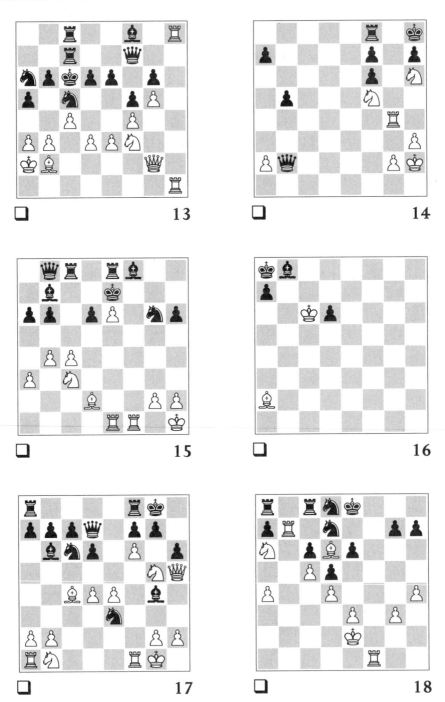

13

14

15

16

17

18

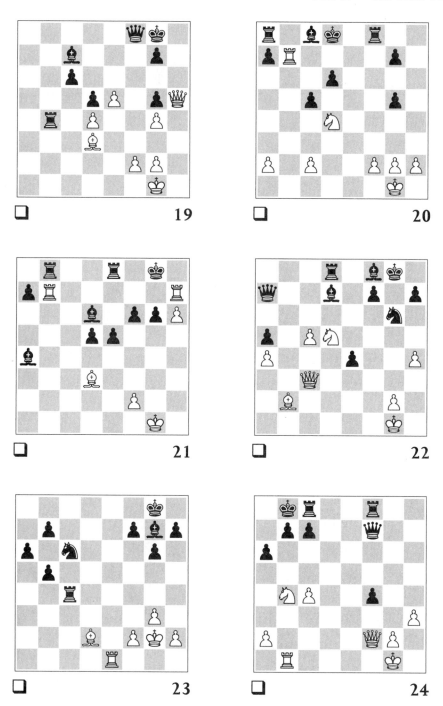

19

20

21

22

23

24

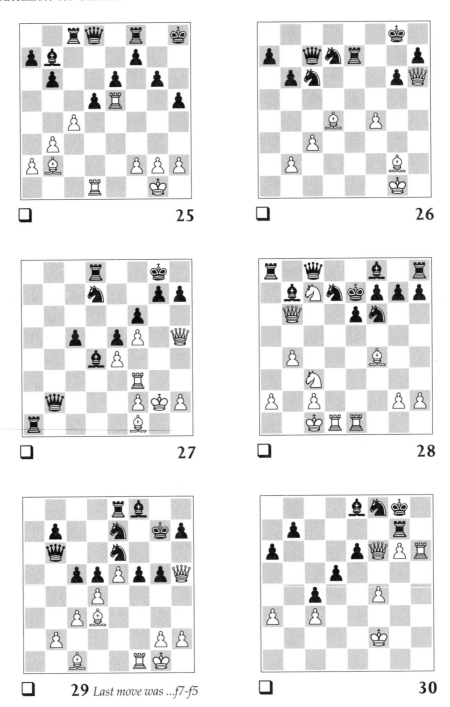

❑ **25**

❑ **26**

❑ **27**

❑ **28**

❑ **29** *Last move was ...f7-f5*

❑ **30**

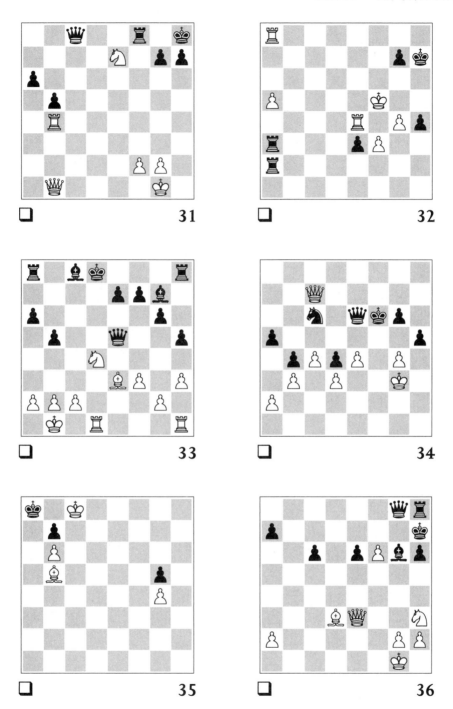

❏   31

❏   32

❏   33

❏   34

❏   35

❏   36

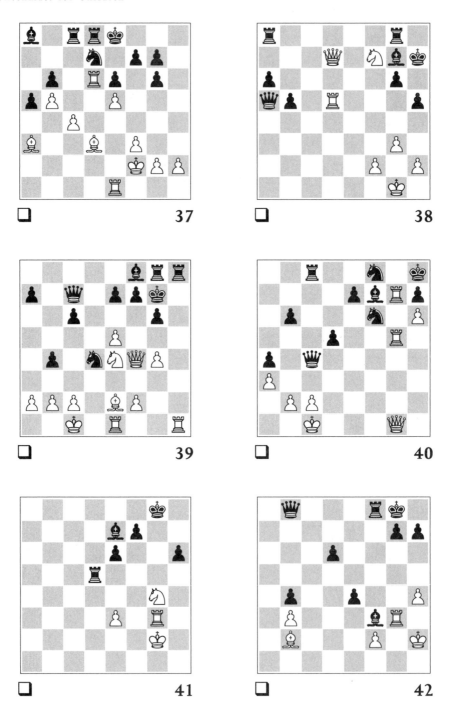

37

38

39

40

41

42

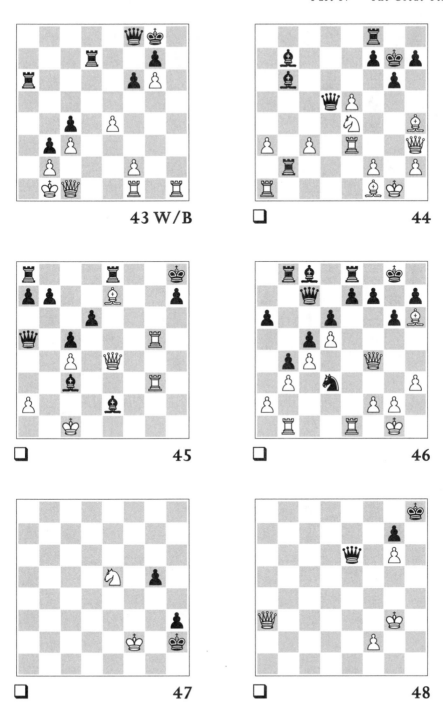

43 W/B

❑ 44

❑ 45

❑ 46

❑ 47

❑ 48

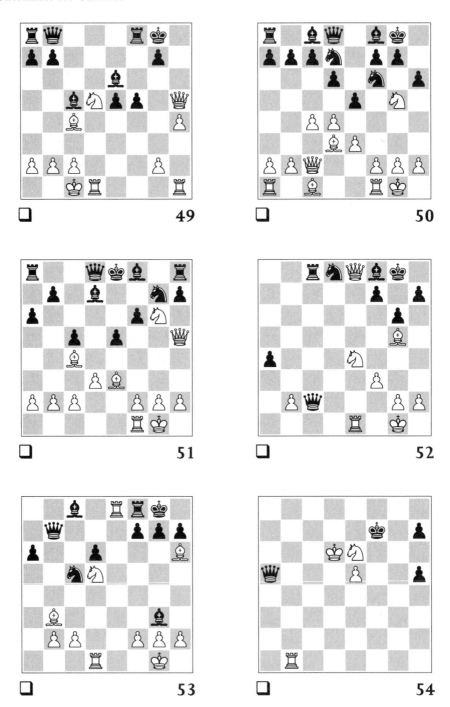

49

50

51

52

53

54

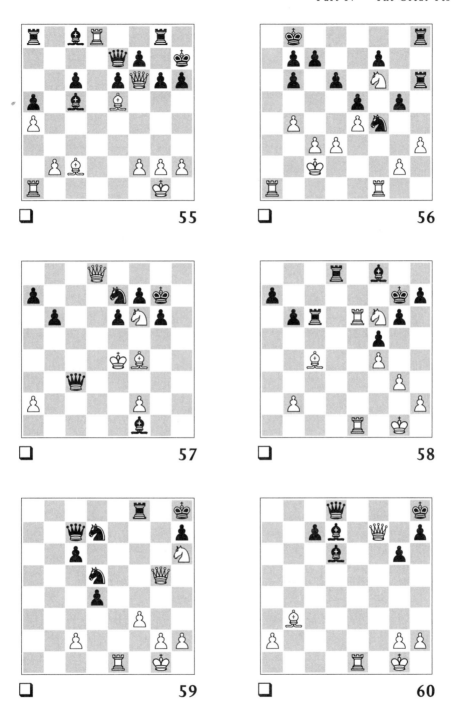

❑ 55

❑ 56

❑ 57

❑ 58

❑ 59

❑ 60

Solutions to 'The Great Test'

Please play through the entire solution, do not only look at the first move or the main variation! The other variations and comments will provide you with important additional knowledge! On the right you will find the points that can be gained for every correct answer. The second number in a field indicates additional points that can be gained. Numbers between brackets (e.g. 2) indicate points that can be scored for alternative solutions.

1	Black can defend against **1.♕a3-f8+** with **1...♘f6-g8**, but not against the mate with **2.♕f8-g7#**.	2
2	An unprotected rook should not be a hindrance for a mating attack. And to give mate with two rooks, you are not always obliged to make a rook move. Here **1.♔a3-b4#** does the job; it opens the a-file and protects the rook on b5 as well!	1
3	After the queen attacks with **1.♕g4-c8+**, a mating position is immediately established: **1...♔a8-a7 2.♕c8xb7#**.	2
4	**1.♖f4-f7+** forces the king into a dead end street, and after **1...♔h7-h6**, **2.♖f8-h8#** brings on the mate.	2
5	Both queens can give mate from a distance: White: **1.♕g5-d8#** Black: **1...♕b4-e1#**	1 1
6	There are three possibilities for White: **1.♔a4-b3** is the best, as it immediately creates a mating position: **1...♔a1-b1 2.♕b4-e1#**. The worst option is *1.♔a4-a3??* with stalemate! Adequate, though time-consuming, is **1.♕b4-d2** *♔a1-b1* 2.♔a4-b3 *♔b1-a1* and now e.g. 3.♕d2-b2#. For 1.♔b3 we give 2 points, for 1.♕d2 1 point, and for 1.♔a3 – please don't ask!	2 (1)
7	**1.♖f3-h3+** and now either **1...♔h7-g6**, which is met by **2.♗c6-e4#**, or **1...♔h7-g8**, but this doesn't change the fact that the king is caught: **2.♗c6-d5#**.	2

8	On **1.♕h3-h8+** Black can easily defend with **1...♞f6-g8**, but now the bishop comes into play, forcing the decision against the immobile king with **2.♗e3-h6#**.	2
9	The position looks much more complicated than it actually is. Do not be distracted by the multitude of pieces – most of them do not play any part. The rook pair and the knight pair are in action here! The ♖c1 protects the ♞c7, which cuts off the escape square e8. The ♖d1 pins the d6 pawn, and this allows **1.♞f3xe5#**.	2
10	White does not have to worry about the attack on his queen. The double check **1.♞f7-d6++** introduces a Smothered Mate: **1...♚e8-d8 2.♕h5-e8+ ♖h8xe8** and now **3.♞d6-f7#**.	3
11	The possibility of mate on h7 is easy to see. Unfortunately, the stupid knight is in the way. White could try to start a mating attack with the queen, but 1.♕h2-g3 is easily parried. In such cases we must get rid of the obstructing knight (and clear the file). This is done here with **1.♞h5-f6+** and now we win by **1...g7xf6** [or 1...♚g8-h8] **2.♕h2xh7#**.	2
12	Do you remember our little 'excursion' into **double check**? This is also the trick that decides the issue here, even though the white queen is under attack. Against the two checks given by **1.♞e4-f6#** there is no defence, even though either of them separately would be easy to parry. For the other double check **1.♞e4-d6++** you get no points. Not only does White squander a great chance with this move, he also loses a piece. There could follow: 1...♚e8-d7 and now 2.♕e2xf3 ♗f8xd6 3.♕f3-g4+ (or 3.♕f3xb7 ♞b8-c6) 3...♚d7-e8 4.♕g4xg7 and Black saves his rook with 4...♕d8-f6.	2
13	And because it's such a pretty sight, here's another dangerous double check with mate. Here it is again, a little hidden between all those pieces, but hopefully the fact that the black king and the white queen are on the same diagonal has caught your attention. And indeed this is deadly after **1.♞f3-e5#**.	1

14	The Arab Mate is not possible here, but still White starts with **1.♖g4-g8+**, because after the forced **1...♖f8xg8**, **2.♘h6xf7#** wins against the boxed-in king in the corner.	2
15	This time the rook achieves an epaulette mate – with quite broad yokes indeed: **1.♖f1-f7+ ♔e7-d8 2.♖f7-d7#**	2
16	**1.♗a2-d5** forces Black to play **1...a7-a5/a6** [On 1...♗b8-c7, 2.♔c6xc7# wins], vacating the b6-square for the white king, who opens the bishop diagonal at the same time with his discovery and thus wins: **2.♔c6-b6#**	2
17	'No use trying to scare me!' is the motto here. **1.♕h5-g6** exploits the pin on the f7 pawn. Black cannot prevent both threatened mates, e.g. **1...♘e3xc4 2.♕g6-h7/xg7#**.	3
18	The difficulty is always that you should not only command a view of the position at hand, but also of the one that will arise after one move. Here, the ♘d7 blocks the 7th rank for the ♖b7. But with **1.♖f1-f8+ ♘d7xf8** the rank is emptied, and now **2.♖b7-e7#** is possible. Always try to get a clear view of the most important changes that your move or your opponent's move creates. This way you will often discover amazing possibilities!	2
19	Queen + Bishop versus a king that cannot escape to the side – that should be a piece of cake (except if you play ♕h5-h7+, as then the king escapes via f7): **1.♗d3-h7+ ♔g8-h8 2.♗h7-g6+** With the discovered check White blocks the future escape square f7. And now: **2...♔h8-g8 3.♕h5-h7#**. A more laborious plan would be (*1.♗d3-h7+ ♔g8-h8*) **2.♗h7-f5+ ♔h8-g8 3.♗f5-e6+ ♕f8-f7 4.♕h5xf7+ ♔g8-h7 5.♕f7-h5#**. If you have seen both, you get 5 points!	3 (2)
20	The rook and the knight are under attack, but still this position is winning for White: **1.♘d4-c6+ ♔d8-e8**, and thanks to the black rook, which blocks the escape route for its king, White can play **2.♖b7-e7#**. What would be different if there were a black knight instead of the bishop on c8?	2

	The mate square e7 would then be protected, so mate would not be possible, but **1.♘d4-e6+ ♚d8-e8 2.♘e6xg7+ ♚e8-d8 3.♘g7-e6+** etc. would secure White a draw by perpetual check! He could even play on for a win with 3.♘g7-e6+ ♚d8-e8 4.♘e6-c7+ ♚e8-d8 5.♘c7xa8	2
21	The two rooks on the 7th rank alone would not achieve more than a draw by perpetual check. But since the pawn on h6 can protect one of them, the mate is quite easy: **1.♖b7-g7+ ♚g8-f8 2.♖h7-h8#**.	2
22	The Queen/Bishop battery is eyeing two possible mate squares, viz. g7 and h8. One of these squares is guarded by the black bishop, the other by the knight, so one of these guards must be removed. This is done with **1.♘d5-e7+**, and now either **1...♗f8xe7 2.♕c3-g7#** or **1...♘g6xe7 2.♕c3-h8#**. On the other hand, the apparently logical *1.h4-h5?* does not work on account of 1...♕a7xc5+ – this even results in a winning position for Black. With **1.♘d5-f6+ ♚g8-g7 2.♘f6xd7+ ♚g7-g8 3.♘d7-f6+ ♚g8-g7 4.♘f6xe4+ ♚g7-g8 5.♘e4-f6+**etc. White can only achieve perpetual check.	2
23	**1.♖e1-e8+ ♗g7-f8 2.♗d2-h6** White attacks the pinned bishop. Black plays any move [A last trick would be 2...♖c4-e4, but only a beginner would allow that to distract him] and then **3.♖e8xf8#**.	3
24	*1.♘b4xa6+* exploits the pin on the b7 pawn and wins a pawn. Nice for White! But much, much stronger is **1.♘b4-c6+**, which also exploits the pin, but at the same time enables **1...♚b8-a8 2.♕f2-a7#**. Do not immediately strike to get a small advantage – first look if there is more in the position!	2 (0.5)
25	White has no queen, but his ♗b2 controls the long diagonal. This is always dangerous, especially when the king is standing on it, thus allowing a discovered check or even a double check: **1.♖e5xh5+ ♚h8-g8 2.♖h5-h8#** A typical Corner Mate with Bishop + Rook.	2

26	The black rook prevents the threatened mate on g7. But after **1.♗g2-d5+ ♖e7-f7** it is pinned, and we know that a pinned piece cannot protect anything. White exploits this with **2.♕h6-g7#**.	2
27	You have to know two mating motifs to solve this exercise. **1.♗f1-c4+** [1...♔g8-f8 2.♕h5-f7#] is the first. If Black, as can be expected, does not fall for this, the second motif applies: **1...♔g8-h8 2.♕h5xh7+** Motif: 'mate on the h-file, bishop cuts off the escape square'. **2...♔h8xh7 3.♖f3-h3#**	4
28	A double double check is definitely not an everyday occurrence. With **1.♗f4-d6+ ♔e7-d8** the starting position for the first double check is reached. **2.♘c7xe6+ ♔d8-e8** and the second double check allows the king no way out: **3.♘e6xg7#**	5
29	Hopefully you have been warned by the clue given under the diagram. White can take the f5 pawn en passant and thus open the diagonal for his bishop, clearing the way for a mating attack: **1.e5xf6 ♔g7-g8 2.♕h5xh7#**	2
30	To solve this exercise, you must know the manoeuvre of Queen versus Rook and King in the corner, which is here introduced with a diversionary sacrifice: **1.♖h6-h8+ ♔g8xh8 2.♕f6xf8+ ♖g7-g8 3.♕f8-h6#** Once again the queen has outplayed the rook, which cannot keep up with her in small spaces.	3
31	Lightning strikes from a distance, in the shape of a queen on h7: **1.♕b1xh7+ ♔h8xh7 2.♖b4-h4#** and the so-called **'Anastasia's Mate'** ends the game (this mate is known from a mating position in the book 'Anastasia and the chess game', which was published long ago). This is one of those mating motifs where it is very important to see the entire board, not only the part where 'things are happening'!	2
32	You have to calculate a little further to see the mate here. And a 'quiet move' must be calculated, which does not give check and doesn't even threaten anything, but helps create the mating position: **1.♖a8-h8+ ♔h7xh8 2.♔f5-g6** Keeping the black king cornered, where he is in a mate position. None of his pieces can help him: **2...♖a3xa5 3.♖e4-e8#**	4

33	'Hopefully he will play for the win of the queen', the black player was probably hoping and praying here. No, he hadn't lost his mind, but he had seen that after the surprising **1.♘d4-e6+ ♚d8-e8** there follows the back-rank mate (with an 'Arab' touch) **2.♖d1-d8#**. *1.♘d4-c6+* does win the queen, but leads to a worse and probably losing endgame: 1...♚d8-c7 2.♘c6xe5 ♝g7xe5 etc. – for this you get 0 points!	3

34	**1.g4-g5+** lures the king into a mating net: **1...♚f6xg5 2.♕c7-f4#**
	Since this was quite easy, we have two additional questions:
	  a) Where should a bishop be in order for Black to be mated in the starting position?
	  b) Where should a knight be in order for Black to be mated in the starting position?
	Solution E1 is given after Solution 60.
		2
		
		1
		
		1

35	Passed pawns should be given free passage by any means, especially if a boxed-in enemy king is close by: **1.♝b5-a6** Zugzwang. Black has to capture. But not having to capture wouldn't help either, as then ♝a6xb7# would follow. **1...b7xa6 2.b6-b7+ ♚a8-a7 3.b7-b8♕#**	3
36	You can choose between two roads to mate: **1.♘h3-g5+ h6xg5** Opening the file, and now the boxed-in king is helpless against **2.♕e3-h3#**. The white attack also rolls via the other flank: **1.♕e3xa7+ ♕g8-f7**, and since the ♝g6 is pinned, the queen is unprotected and can simply be captured: **2.♕a7xf7#**. For each winning line you get 2 points and if you have seen both, you can enjoy 4 points!	2 2
37	Kudos to the reader who has recognized the two-bishop mate and introduced it with **1.♖d6xe6+! f7xe6 2.♝d3xg6#** On a full board it is often hard to recognize such known mating patterns in time.	3

38	The mating motif is not easy to see here, as the black king position appears to be solid. But after **1.♖d5xh5+ g6xh5** [or 1...♗g7-h6 2.♘f7-g5+ (double check) 2...♔h7-h8 3.♖h5xh6# or 3.♕d7-h7#] **2.♕d7-f5/d3#** his own pieces are standing in the way of the king, and the knight blocks the rest of the escape squares. We should always take a closer look if the opponent has a confined king – often there are amazing tactical possibilities to be found!	3
39	Do not be afraid to make big sacrifices if you see a mating motif! Here the king is surrounded by his own pieces, and he is cut off from the h-file by the white rook. Thus, White can use his queen to eliminate the most important defender, the e7 pawn: **1.♕f4-f6+ e7xf6 2.e5xf6#**	2
40	If most of the pieces were cleared off the board, it would be much easier to see the mating motif with ♕g7. You should not let a multitude of pieces – and certainly not your own pieces – cloud your vision! Here White simply clears away all the obstacles: **1.♖g7-g8+ ♗f7xg8 2.♖g5xg8+ ♘f6xg8 3.♕g1-g7#**	4
41	The double check **1.♘g4-f6++** does not lead to the win of an exchange, but to an Arab Mate. Whether Black plays 1...♔g8-f8 or 1...♔g8-h8, White always replies **2.♖g3-g8#**.	2
42	The manoeuvre **1.♖g3xg7+ ♔g8-h8 2.♖g7-g6+** shouldn't have been hard to find. Here it does not matter to which square on the g-file the rook moves – in other positions, where Black can interpose pieces, this may be different. Therefore, do not play schematically – look carefully if your mate plan is feasible! **2...♖f8-f6 2.♗b2xf6#**	3
43	'The Pharmacist's dream', we could call this exercise, as Damiano's mating recipe functions on both sides here. (Granted, this is a constructed position – in practice this is very, very rare.) The plan is identical for both sides, and it is easy: get rid of the rook(s) with check, and give mate with the queen on h7 (a2). **1.♖h1-h8+ ♔g8xh8 2.♖f1-h1+ ♔h8-g8 3.♖h1-h8+ ♔g8xh8 4.♕c1-h1+ ♔h8-g8 5.♕h1-h7#** *If Black were to move*, White would get mated with 1...♖a6-a1+ 2.♔b1xa1 ♕f8-a8+ 3.♔a1-b1 ♕a8-a2#. For one solution you get 5 points; if you have found the solution for both Black and White you get 2 additional points.	5
		2

44	One and the same move introduces two different mating patterns: **1.♗h4-f6+ ♔g7-g8 2.♕h3-h6** Black any, and now **3.♕h6-g7#** is the tried-and-tested method to exploit the fianchetto hole. Instead, **2.♕h3xh7+** builds on the mating motif with Rook + Bishop in the corner: 2...♔g8xh7 3.♖e3-h3+ ♔h7-g8 4.♖h3-h8#. For each variation you get 3 points, and if you have seen both, this will even net you 6 points. It is not so important whether one mate takes one move more or less than the other. It is important that it can be carried through by force and with as few uncertainties as possible, which is the case in both variations here.	3 3
45	If the king is cut off from the g-file – if his only protection is provided by the h7 pawn – if the opponent has brought on all his major pieces and the defenders are standing offside – then it is time for the 'Two-Rook Mate': **1.♕e4xh7+ ♔h8xh7 2.♖g3-h3+ ♗e2-h5 3.♖h2xh5#**	3
46	White can ignore the knight fork, since two mating motifs are working for him. The pin on the e7 pawn enables White to play: **1.♕f4-f6** and now either **1...e7xf6 2.♖e1xe8#** or **1...♘d3xe1** (or other moves) **2.♕f6-g7#**: either mate with Queen + Bishop on g7, or a Back-Rank Mate with Rook + Bishop.	4
47	Zugzwang is the key to the win: **1.♘e5-g4+ ♔h2-h1 2.♔f2-f1** Now only the h-pawn can move – and it deprives its king of his escape square! **2...h3-h2 3.♘g4-f2#** Without zugzwang, this position could not be won, the king could simply move from h1 to h2 and back.	4
48	This position is a simple win, if White commands a view of the entire board. However, beginners have a strong tendency to look only at the direct sphere of action and not see the whole width of the board: **1.♕a3-f8+ ♕e6-g8 2.♕f8-f5 ♕g8-b8+**, and Black will escape the mating attack. If you know how to use the entire board, you will win with **1.♕a3-a8+ ♕e6-g8 2.♕a8-h1+ ♕g8-h7 3.♕h1xh7#**.	4

49	Queen and Bishop could achieve mate here, but their own knight prevents this. Here only a clearance sacrifice helps, and **1.♘d5-e7+** clears the diagonal. **1...♗c5xe7 2.♗c4xe6+ ♖f8-f7 3.♕h5xf7+ ♚g8-h8 4.♕f7-h5#** The laborious **3.♗e6xf7+** also wins, however it is weaker: 3...♚g8-f8 4.♗f7-c4 ♗e7-g5+ 5.h4xg5 ♕b8-c7 and White achieves the mate one move later. For that you will only get 3 points.	5 (3)
50	After **1.♗d3-h7+** the king has an escape square: **1...♚g8-h8**, and in many positions he would be safe now. However, here the f7-square is unprotected, which changes everything: **2.♘g5xf7#**. **1...♘f6xh7** does not help Black either, since now the h7-square is not protected by the ♘f6 any more, and the bishop, which was in the way of its queen, has gone. This allows **2.♕c2xh7#**.	3
51	Especially in the opening, when the king is still surrounded by his pieces, three minor pieces are often worth much more than a queen. That is why here White sacrifices the queen for a victorious attack with minor pieces: **1.♘g6xh8+ ♘g7xh5 2.♗c4-f7+ ♚e8-e7 3.♗e3xc5#** [*1.♘g6xe5+* wins in the same way: 1...♘g7xh5 (1...♚e8-e7 2.♗e3xc5#) 2.♗c4-f7+ ♚e8-e7 3.♗e3xc5#]	5
52	The obvious move **1.♗g5-h6** does give White an advantage: 1...♘d8-e6 2.♘e4-f6+ ♚g8-h8 3.♕e8xf7 ♗f8-g7 etc. But it does not lead to mate. White has another way to win: **1.♘e4-f6+ ♚g8-g7** and now the queen sacrifice **2.♕e8xf8+** produces an already known mating picture: **2...♚g7xf8 3.♗g5-h6#**	4
53	With **1.♘d5-e7+** White could win the queen, and after 1...♕b7xe7 (1...♚g8-h8?? 2.♖e8xf8#) 2.♖e8xe7 the game would be approximately equal. Not bad. But even better is **1.♘d5-f6+**. Then Black is forced to open the small diagonal for the bishop with **1...g7xf6**, and now you will surely see the already known mating motif with **2.♖e8xf8#**. The only other move, 1...♚g8-h8, loses simply to 2.♖e8xf8#. For 1.♘e7+ you get 1 point, for 1.♘f6+ you get 2 points. If you have found both solutions, you can even write 3 points!	2 (2)

54	White's only chance is to attack the enemy king. But there is only one good way to do this. The knight cannot do much, and the rook cannot achieve mate on the 7th or 8th rank. That leaves the f-file: **1.♖b1-f1+** a) **1...♔f7-e8/g8 2.♖f1-f8#** On b) **1...♔f7-g6** there follows 2.♖f1-f6#. The knight and Black's own pawns block all four escape squares. For the complete solution you get 3 points. But this means you should have seen both mate variations! Otherwise, you get 1 point for a), and 2 for b).	**3**
55	Has the corner square h8 caught your eye? We know this from the mating motifs with Bishop + Rook or Queen! Only, you should not allow yourself to be irritated or distracted. Just like the queen and bishop, the ♖d8 is eyeing h8 − 'through' the black rook. And so, **1.♕f6-h8+ ♖g8xh8 2.♖d8xh8#** decides the issue.	**3**
56	To lure the king into the corner and then give mate is a really tempting idea. Alas, he will escape after **1.♖a1-a8+ ♔b8xa8 2.♖f1-a1+ ♔a8-b8 3.♘f6-d7+ ♔b8-c8.** A small transposition solves this problem: (1.♖a1-a8+ ♔b8xa8) and now first **2.♘f6-d7**, which blocks the escape route for the king. Black plays any move, and now **3.♖f1-a1#.** A move order that does not lead to the desired result may be made to function by changing the order of two moves, as here, or by inserting a zwischenzug [Has this term already been explained? If not, will readers know what it means? - SWG]. A little fantasy and talent for combinations is needed, and then many a victory can be achieved!	**4**
57	Although this exercise can be solved in two or three moves, it may well be one of the toughest of this test. With the queen sacrifice **1.♕d8-f8+ ♔g7xf8 2.♗f4-h6#** White creates a Bishop + Knight Mate. Of course Black can decline the sacrifice, but that does not help him either: 1...♔g7xf6 2.♕f8-h8# **1.♗f4-h6+** is a somewhat more complicated solution: 1...♔g7xh6 (1...♔g7xf6 2.♕d8-h8#) 2.♕d8-h8+ ♔h6-g5 and now the f-pawn decides: 3.f2-f4#. For this solution there are 5 points, even if you have not found the shortest way. If you have found both solutions, you can be proud of yourself and net 9 points!	**4** **5**

58	This exercise contains many interesting mating motifs. The key move is **1.♖e6-e7+**. Whether Black captures or not, mate follows in all cases: **1...♗f8xe7** [*1...♔g7xf6* 2.♖e7-f7# Mate with Rook + Bishop, supported by the f4 pawn; or *1...♔g7-h6* 2.♖e7xh7# An Arab Mate with support by the f4 pawn. (If you have not seen this, you had the additional possibility of 2.♘f6-g8+ ♔h6-h5 3.♗c4-e2#.)] **2.♖e1xe7+ ♔g8-h8** [2...♔g7-f8 3.♖e7-f7# Mate with Rook, Bishop, Knight] and now the Arab Mate **3.♖e7-h7#**.	5
59	**1.♖e1-e8!** [1...♖f8xe8 fails to 2.♘h6-f7#; in an unchanged position the threat is 2.♘h6-f7# as well as 2.♖e8xf8+ ♘d7xf8 3.♕g5-g8#] **1...♕c7-f4** seems to clear up the situation, but now White tosses off a third mating motif: **2.♕g5-g8+ ♖f8xg8 3.♖e8xg8#** The ♖e8 controlled the g8-square 'through' its counterpart. Thus g8 was attacked by the queen, the knight and the rook, and protected by the king and the rook only.	5
60	We conclude with another seemingly quite difficult exercise. This is sure to provoke a little wishful thinking in many a reader: 'If only the ♗d7 weren't there, I could play ♖e8+, or: 'If I had a dark-squared bishop, I could give mate on the long diagonal'. My friends, you have everything you need – you should just employ it in the right way! **1.♖e1-e8+** is possible despite the ♗d7, since after **1...♗d7xe8** the queen's protection of g8 is cut off (we call this '**line closure**' or '**line interference**') and the simple mate **2.♕f7-g8#** becomes possible. **1...♕d8xe8** will give you the craved-for dark-squared bishop, albeit in the shape of the queen in this case. But we know that this makes no difference. Therefore: **2.♕f7-f6#**.	4
E1	a) This was a trick question – the bishop cannot give mate anywhere! On ♗h4 there simply follows g6-g5, and ♗h8/g7 leaves the king the escape square g5.	1
	b) **♘h7#** Giving check and at the same time controlling the escape square g5.	1

My Solutions, My Points

	Solution	Pts.		Solution	Pts.
1			31		
2			32		
3			33		
4			34		
5			35		
6			36		
7			37		
8			38		
9			39		
10			40		
11			41		
12			42		
13			43		
14			44		
15			45		
16			46		
17			47		
18			48		
19			49		
20			50		
21			51		
22			52		
23			53		
24			54		
25			55		
26			56		
27			57		
28			58		
29			59		
30			60		

Half-time score: Final score:

Evaluation

50 points or less	You have had a lot of trouble coping with the transition from the illustrative examples and quiz exercises to the more difficult exercises from practice. Now be honest with yourself: Could it be that you have worked through Parts I and II too casually? If yes, have another careful look at them, and also at the material that we suggest one page further on, e.g. the Gaffron series. Then do this test one more time. Don't lose heart, you will get there in the end!
51-90 points	That was not bad to begin with, but surely you can do still better! Have another look at the exercises that you haven't managed to solve. Do they have something in common? Perhaps it is the longer variations, or a certain motif (e.g. double check), or something else that has taken you a lot of effort? If yes, have another good look at it.
91-130 points	If you have scored more than half of the possible points, you clearly know quite a lot about the art of giving mate! And if you have come so far, you can do better still. Try to approach the exercises with even more concentration, do not get distracted from the motifs and plans by the multitude of material on the board! If you manage that, you will be even better able to convert your knowledge into test points – and eventually into victories on the board!
131-160 points	A very good result! Achieving more than two-thirds of all possible points proves that you have really understood the material. Do not grieve about points you haven't scored – even experienced players will not solve all the exercises correctly. You will surely have learned many additional things from the exercises that you didn't solve.
161 and more points	Congratulations – a truly terrific performance! Many experienced club players could not do better! Clearly you have a lot of talent for chess, and you should further develop this talent with more training.

Additional Material and Tools

Unfortunately, a book has only limited space and the author cannot deal with everything as extensively as he would want to. That is why we have made a list of some recommended additional material you can work with, which can serve to complete and extend this book, or help you with further training.

Sergey Ivashchenko, 'The Manual of Chess Combinations' (1997). Figurine notations, short text in four languages.
Fred Reinfeld, 'How to Force Checkmate' unfortunately still in descriptive notation, includes mate in 1, 2 and 3 moves with short comments.
Bruce Pandolfini, 'The Winning Way', Fireside (1998) is also a good choice.
Josh Waitzkin, 'Attacking Chess', Fireside (1995), which includes a little more text and a number of examples from Waitzkin's prodigy days.

We can recommend the following books for further or additional reading:

Frank Oltman, '1, 2, 3 und Matt!' (i.e. '1, 2, 3 and mate!') and also, by the same author, the brochure '3-Zirkel-Training' (i.e. '3-Circle Training'). We have already made a brief acquaintance with these themes in Part III. Unfortunately these publications are not yet available in English language.
Heinz Brunthaler, 'My Daily Exercise, Volume 1: From Beginner to Club Player', a book that is recommended for players who do not have much time, but would like to do a little training on a regular basis. Each day one commented chess exercise must be solved, and after some time this will provide you with an extensive knowledge of chess tactics.

If you want to improve in chess, you can only accomplish this by training. Practical play is important, but without additional training there will be no real progress!

Glossary of Terms

Attack
When a piece is threatened by capture or a king is threatened by checkmate.

Back rank
The first rank (for White) or the eighth rank (for Black) on the board.

Capture
When a piece is removed by an enemy piece, which then takes the place of the captured piece.

Castling
A move by king and rook that serves to bring the former into safety and to activate the latter. The king is moved sideways two squares from its original square. At the same time, a rook moves from its original square to the adjacent square on the other side of the king. Castling can take place either to the queenside or to the kingside. It is the only way in chess of moving two pieces in one turn. A player may only castle if both the king and rook in question have not moved before in the game, if his king is not in check, and if his king does not pass a square on which it would be in check.

Check
When a king is under direct attack by an opposing piece. A check can be countered either by moving the king, or capturing the piece that gives the check, or by placing a piece between the king and the piece that gives check.

Checkmate
When a king is under direct attack by an opposing piece and there is no way to deal with the threat.

Clearance
When a square, rank, file or diagonal is vacated in such a way that another piece can occupy it.

Combination
A clever and more or less forced sequence of moves which usually results in an advantage for the player who starts the sequence.

Decoy
When a piece is lured (e.g. by a sacrifice) towards a square on which it can be attacked or, in the case of a king, checked and/or mated.

Deflection/Diversion
When a piece is forced to abandon the protection of an important square, file, rank or diagonal.

Diagonal
A line of squares running from top left to bottom right or the other way round (e.g. 'the a1-h8 diagonal').

Discovered attack/check
When a piece is removed in such a way that a piece of the same colour standing behind it, attacks an enemy piece, or, in case of a discovered check, the enemy king.

Double attack

When one piece is attacked by two enemy pieces at the same time, or when one piece attacks two enemy pieces at the same time (for the latter, see also fork).

Double check

When a king is attacked by two enemy pieces at the same time (by means of a discovered check). A double check can only be countered by a king move.

Endgame/Ending

The final phase of the game when there are few pieces left on the board.

En passant

When a pawn which has just moved forward two squares from its original square, is captured by an enemy pawn standing immediately beside it. This capturing pawn then occupies the square behind the captured pawn, as if it had made a normal capture.

Exchange

1) When both sides capture pieces that are of equal value. A synonym is 'trading' or 'swapping' pieces.
2) The surplus in value of a rook above a minor piece (bishop or knight). The player who possesses the rook is 'an exchange up', he has 'won the exchange'.

Fianchetto

The development of a bishop to the second square of the adjacent file of the knight (to b2 or g2 for White, to b7 or g7 for Black).

File

A line of squares from the top to the bottom of the board (e.g. 'the e-file').

Fork

When two (or more) pieces are attacked simultaneously by the same opposing piece.

Kingside

The board half on the right (from the white player's point of view, i.e. the e-, f-, g- and h-files).

Luft

When a pawn is moved forward to create an escape possibility for its own king.

Major piece

A queen or a rook.

Mate

See Checkmate.

Mating net

A situation where a king is attacked by enemy pieces and eventually cannot escape the mate threat.

Middlegame

The phase of the game that follows immediately after the opening.

Minor piece

A bishop or a knight.

Open file/rank/diagonal

A rank, file or diagonal whose squares are not occupied by pieces or pawns.

Opening

The initial phase of the game.

Overburdening/Overload

When a piece has to protect more than one fellow piece or square at the same time and is not able to maintain this situation satisfactorily.

Passed pawn

A pawn that has no enemy pawns on the same or an adjacent file. Its promotion can only be prevented by enemy pieces.

Perpetual (check)

An unstoppable series of checks that neither player can avoid without risking a loss. This means that the game ends in a draw.

Piece

In general, all chessmen apart from the pawns. In this book, mostly queen, rook, bishop and knight are meant because many tactical motifs (sacrifices, for instance) cannot be carried out by a king.

Pin

An attack on a piece that cannot move away without exposing a more valuable piece behind it. Pins can take place on a rank, file or diagonal.

Promotion

When a pawn reaches the back rank, it is turned into a more valuable piece (queen, rook, bishop or knight).

Queenside

The board half on the left (from the white player's point of view, i.e. the a-, b-, c- and d-files).

Rank

A line of squares running from side to side (e.g. 'the third rank').

Sacrifice

When material is deliberately given up for other gains.

Square

One of the 64 sections on the chess board that can be occupied by a pawn, piece or king.

Stalemate

When a player who is not in check has no legal move and it is his turn. This means that the game ends in a draw.

Tempo

The duration of one move made by one side. A tempo can be won or deliberately lost by several methods.

Underpromotion

The promotion of a pawn to a piece of lesser value than the queen. This is quite rare.

Wing

Either the kingside or the queenside.

Zugzwang

When a player is to move and he cannot do anything without making an important concession.

Zwischenschach

Intermediate check, disrupting a logical sequence of moves.

Zwischenzug

Intermediate move with a point that disrupts a logical sequence of moves.

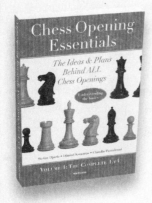
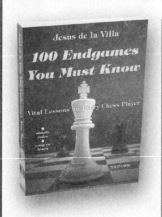